The Twin Children of the Holocaust

Stolen Childhood and the Will to Survive

Nancy L. Segal

Foreword by David G. Marwell

Photographs From the Twins
40TH Anniversary Reunion at Auschwitz-Birkenau

BOSTON
2023

*For the Twins Whose Lives Were Irreparably Altered
by Horrific Events at Auschwitz-Birkenau,*

and

the Twins Whose Lives Were Lost—

We Remember You

Library of Congress Cataloging-in-Publication Data

Names: Segal, Nancy L., 1951- author.
Title: The twin children of the Holocaust : stolen childhoods and the will
  to survive, photographs from the twins' 40th anniversary reunion at
Auschwitz-Birkenau / Nancy L. Segal.
Other titles: Stolen childhoods and the will to survive, pictures from the
  twins' 40th anniversary reunion at Auschwitz-Birkenau
Description: Boston : Cherry Orchard Books, 2023. | Includes
  bibliographical references.
Identifiers: LCCN 2022049348 (print) | LCCN 2022049349 (ebook) |
  ISBN 9798887190860 (paperback) | ISBN 9798887190877 (adobe pdf) |
  ISBN 9798887190884 (epub)
Subjects: LCSH: Jewish children in the Holocaust—Pictorial works. | Jewish
  children in the Holocaust—History. | Holocaust, Jewish
  (1939-1945)—Pictorial works. | Holocaust, Jewish (1939-1945)—History.
  | Twins—Poland—Pictorial works. | Auschwitz (Concentration
  camp)—Pictorial works. | Birkenau (Concentration camp)—Pictorial
  works. | Human experimentation in medicine—History—20th century. |
  CYAC: Holocaust survivors—Pictorial works.
Classification: LCC D804.48 .S443 2023 (print) | LCC D804.48 (ebook) |
  DDC 940.53/18083—dc23/eng/20221018
LC record available at https://lccn.loc.gov/2022049348
LC ebook record available at https://lccn.loc.gov/2022049349

ISBN 9798887190860 (paperback)
ISBN 9798887190877 (adobe pdf)
ISBN 9798887190884 (epub)

Book design by Tatiana Vernikov
Cover design by Ivan Grave

Published by Cherry Orchard Books, and imprint of Academic Studies Press
1577 Beacon St.
Brookline, MA 02446, USA
press@academicstudiespress.com
www.academicstudiespress.com

Contents

Foreword by David G. Marwell   7

Preface   10
1. Minneapolis to Auschwitz and Jerusalem: How Did it Happen?   12
2. Pre-event Activities: Meeting Twins   16
3. Traveling to Poland   19
4. Visiting Auschwitz-Birkenau: Reunion and Re-enactment   22
5. Exploring Auschwitz-Birkenau: An Art Museum,   36
      a Chance Meeting, and a Trip to the Polish Border
6. Medical Experiments: Process and Purpose   49
7. Touring Warsaw: War Memorials and Everyday Life   61
8. Twin Testimonies: Public Hearing on Josef Mengele's War Crimes   67
9. Aftermath: Inquiries and Inquest   90
10. Twin Children of the Holocaust: After the Hearing and Beyond   98

Parting Words   106
Acknowledgments   107
About the Author   108
Other Books by Nancy L. Segal   109

The Twin Children of the Holocaust

Foreword by David G. Marwell

It is one of the many ironies of the story of Josef Mengele and his escape from justice that the first coordinated and effective international search for him should have been launched only after he had been dead for six years. I tell this story in the second half of my recent book, *Mengele:Unmasking the "Angel of Death,"* in which I trace the origins of that investigation which, although it did not locate a living Mengele, led to the discovery of his body and accounted for his whereabouts from the time he left Auschwitz in January 1945 until his death by natural causes on a beach in Brazil in 1979. A second striking irony is that it took the effective efforts of his victims—rather than those of the institutions of justice—to provide the moral and political pressure that impelled the investigation. Those who were exploited precisely because of their powerlessness were able to orchestrate the instruments of power and move governments to action.

The agents of this campaign for justice were the surviving twins of Mengele's experiments, led by Eva Mozes Kor, a real estate agent from Indiana. Aware of the power of publicity and the strategic use of spectacle, Eva played a major role in organizing two events at the beginning of 1985. First was the return to Auschwitz of a group of twins on the 40th anniversary of its liberation, and, shortly thereafter, a mock trial of Josef Mengele in Israel.

Nearly outnumbered by camera crews from around the world, Eva and her fellow twins, including her twin sister Miriam, made the painful return journey to Auschwitz—the place that had changed their lives forever. Eva described to the press how she still suffered under the weight of having "never said goodbye" to her mother. Marc Berkowitz said he was "searching for the child" he was before "this happened." If the trip to Auschwitz represented an emotional tsunami for the twins who made the journey, the mock trial at Yad Vashem provided a searing indictment of the man who embodied the evil that took their families and their childhoods and left an unbounded expanse of physical and emotional pain.

The mock trial was held in conjunction with "The World Convention of Twins and Others Who Underwent Experiments by Mengele." To add pedigree and credibility to the proceeding, key figures in the history of war crimes investigations and prosecution were chosen to serve on the six-member board of inquiry, among them Gideon Hausner, the former Israeli Attorney General and lead prosecutor of Adolph Eichmann; Gen. Telford Taylor, the former American Chief Counsel for War Crimes at Nuremberg; and Simon Wiesenthal, the famed Nazi hunter. The thirty witnesses at the trial included Simone Veil, the Auschwitz survivor and former French minister and President of the European Parliament, and one of the dwarfs who had been subjected to Mengele's experiments, but they were mostly twins. Forty years after the liberation of Auschwitz, dramatic testimony, much of it heard for the first time, detailed the crimes that were perpetrated there. The remarkable event, held at Israel's national Holocaust memorial in Jerusalem over three days in early February 1985, would, it turned out, be the first and only public forum— despite lacking legal authority and the empty dock—available for Mengele's victims to testify about their experience with the man who became known as the Angel of Death.

The story of the twins and their ordeal at the hands of Mengele, which had been movingly described the previous year in a cover story in *Parade Magazine* by the late, crusading reporter Lucette Lagnado, provided a face—or, perhaps better expressed, twin faces—to the crimes of the Nazis and the failure of their victors and victims to have attained justice. This story was crystalized in the twins' traumatic return to Auschwitz and their agonizing testimony at Yad Vashem, and it catalyzed a powerful mixture of politics, pressure, and potent memory that moved those in power to act. It is no accident that on the final day of the mock trial in Jerusalem, U.S. Attorney General William French Smith announced in Washington the launch of the Justice Department's investigation into the "whereabouts of Josef Mengele." Germany, which had carefully followed the planning for the trial, soon joined the U.S. in the investigation as did the State of Israel.

Now, nearly forty years later, thanks to Nancy Segal, we can catch a glimpse for ourselves of these extraordinary gatherings and their assembly of witnesses and memories. Readers should not expect to see carefully composed photographs or artistically rendered images; these are, instead, mostly simple snapshots: the quotidian record of an extraordinary event. It is as if Nancy Segal, who was both witness and chronicler of the twins' journey in 1985, forgot to

retrieve the rolls of film from the drugstore where she dropped them off de-
cades ago, only to pick them up now and share them with us along with her
memories of that historic trip. They are displayed here, providing an eloquent
photographic memory that connects us across time to a truly remarkable slice
of history.

Preface

The Twin Children of the Holocaust: Stolen Childhood and the Will to Survive will have universal meaning for those who care deeply about the injustices and cruelties done to innocent children. Between the Spring 1943 and January 1945, several hundred twins were subjected to unthinkable medical experiments at the Auschwitz-Birkenau death camp. Dr. Josef Mengele was the physician behind the experimentation and other atrocities that involved not just the twins, but also people with various genetic anomalies.

I was privileged to attend the twins' 40th anniversary reunion held at the camp, located in the southern Polish town of Oświęcim, about 45 miles west of Krakow. A record compiled by a prison doctor and bacteriologist forced to work for Mengele showed that 732 pairs of twins were studied;[1] however, estimates have ranged as high as 1,500.[2] It is thought that approximately 200 twins survived, but this estimate has also varied, so it is likely that the exact number will never be known. Having attended the reunion event in Poland I can affirm that only nine twins were present, given the difficulties of obtaining visas and the hardships of winter travel. The nine twins included the members of one complete pair, six individual twins from different pairs, and one non-twin "assigned" as a twin upon arrival; see photograph 6.3. The reunion was followed by a three-day public hearing on Dr. Josef Mengele's war crimes, held at Yad Vashem ("A Memorial and a Name"), the World Holocaust Remembrance Center in Jerusalem, Israel. Many more twins attended this hearing, most likely because a substantial number of them live in Israel.

As I listened to the twins' memories of horror, pain, and fear, I marveled at the clever tricks these young children used and the tall tales they told to unsuspecting officers to obtain extra food, visit a twin sister, or escape from the infirmary. Their resolve and reliance were extraordinary. Whenever possible, they have rebuilt their lives by getting married, raising children, and pur-

---

1   Andy Walker, "The Twins of Auschwitz." *BBC News*, https://www.bbc.com/news/magazine-30933718, January 28, 2015.

2   Jennifer Rosenberg, "A History of Mengele's Gruesome Experiments on Twins." ThoughtCo, https://www.thoughtco.com/mengeles-children-twins-of-auschwitz-1779486, January 1, 2021; Nancy L. Segal (1985). "Holocaust twins: Their special bond." *Psychology Today*, 19 (8), 52-58.

suing productive careers. Virtually all of them believe in the importance of educating the public about what had happened to them at Auschwitz-Birkenau, and have done so through lectures, exhibitions, and films.

I wanted to do my part by publishing the photographs I took thirty-eight years ago, only a fraction of which have been seen by my students, family members, and friends. Many of the pictures I took have languished in binders stored in my university office as I pursued other projects. However, I have become increasingly aware that the twins are a unique minority of the youngest Holocaust survivors who are alive only because being a twin made them valuable to the Nazi doctors; but their number is dwindling. As a psychology professor dedicated to public education—and as a Jewish twin—it is time for me to offer these photographs to those who wish to see them, and to those who need to see them.

I have taken all the photographs in this book, with just a few exceptions that I have noted. The order of presentation is generally, but not strictly, chronological because some pictures were best displayed when grouped together. I believe these pictures speak for themselves, but brief annotation is provided for viewers to fully appreciate their context and meaning.

1. Minneapolis to Auschwitz and Jerusalem: How Did it Happen?

Beginning in the Fall 1982 and for the next nine years, I was a postdoctoral fellow at the University of Minnesota, where I worked on the *Minnesota Study of Twins Reared Apart*. Gathering data from newly reunited identical and fraternal twin pairs was a fascinating task, but my excitement was no match for the pure joy and uncontrolled glee that the reunited twins displayed or described when meeting for the first time. I understood their excitement—as a fraternal twin I was raised alongside my twin sister, Anne, who looks and behaves very differently than I do. We had our differences as children and still do, but we also relish our close companionship, unconditional acceptance, and shared understandings. The situation was far different in Europe during the 1930s and 1940s: the evolving ties of Jewish twins (mostly children) were tragically severed as they became unwitting subjects in Dr. Josef Mengele's horrifying medical experiments after being torn from their families.

I know that as a Jewish twin, had I been born in another time and place, I too, along with Anne, would have been singled out by Nazi officers for study.

I attended both the Auschwitz-Birkenau gathering and the Yad Vashem hearing. This is how it came about. In September 1984, Minnesota twin study director, Professor Thomas J. Bouchard, Jr., chose me to be part of Pat Mitchell's *NBC* televised talk show, *Woman to Woman*, the first such program to be produced and hosted by a woman.[3,4] This meant flying to Los Angeles for the taping, followed by a trip to Disneyland with a California friend, both of which

---

3   The program on twins produced by *Woman to Woman* was broadcast on September 12, 1984. A sample segment from that show can be seen at https://www.youtube.com/watch?v=McUgTQWyviY. *Woman to Woman* was nationally syndicated in 1983-1984 and later became a segment on NBC's *Today Show*. Pat Michell is currently involved in numerous projects focusing on women's issues.

4   Pat E. Mitchell, "Trained by a Life of Change." *New York Times,* https://www.nytimes.com/2013/03/10/jobs/patricia-mitchell-trained-by-a-life-of-change.html?, March 9, 2013.

were enormously appealing. In those days, I had a habit of listening to late night radio and that is how I learned about C.A.N.D.L.E.S. (Children of Auschwitz's Deadly Laboratory Experiments Survivors). C.A.N.D.L.E.S. is the organization of twin Holocaust survivors that would be gathering in Poland, and later in Jerusalem to reclaim the fragments of their young lives, honor deceased relatives and try to bring the former Nazi doctor to justice. At the time, Mengele was believed to be hiding in Paraguay, but that ultimately proved false. I also learned that some twins were attending these events hoping to reunite with their twin brother or twin sister, the primary focus of my work in Minnesota.

Once I heard the news, I *knew* I would be going. I called Professor Bouchard the next day, outlined my plan to go to Poland and he said we would discuss it. But he must have sensed my determination to attend because when I entered his office, he offered me $300 and said, "raise the rest." I headed to the Genetics Institute on campus where then director Jack Sheppard, matched that amount. I was grateful, but I needed additional funding to travel to Poland *and* to purchase a Nikon camera and tape recorder, essential equipment for the activities ahead. My next step was to call the Minneapolis Jewish Federation— and after a single telephone call I was promised $500.

Over the next few weeks, I realized that I must also attend the Yad Vashem hearing in Jerusalem to fully understand and appreciate the twins' life histories. I also realized that this journey required even more financial assistance. I discussed my revised plan with Bouchard who arranged a meeting between the two of us and the late Dr. Norman Garmezy from the University of Minnesota's Child Development Institute. Garmezy was famous for his work with "invulnerable children"[5]—youngsters who thrive despite traumatic and stressful surroundings—but also known for his savvy in navigating collegial connections and opportunities. I will never forget that afternoon. Garmezy raised the idea of contacting psychologist Greg Kimble, a member of the *Psychology Today* Committee. "He owes us a favor!" Garmezy insisted. One of them called Kimble, and I was promised $2,000, contingent upon providing an article for the magazine.[6] I was on my way . . .

---

5   N. Garmezy (1986). "Vulnerable and invulnerable children: Theory, research, and intervention." *Master Lectures on Developmental Psychology*, 137 *Washington, D.C.: American Psychological Association).

6   Nancy L. Segal (1985). "Holocaust twins: Their special bond." *Psychology Today*, 19 (8), 52-58.

1.1. Drawing of twins at Auschwitz-Birkenau. The artist's identity is unknown.
I begin my public and classroom lectures with this slide as it sets the tone
for the pictures that follow. The sketch may depict older twin Zvi Spiegel,
surrounded by the young twin boys; see section 8 and photographs 8.11–8.14.

1.2. This sign was circulated by identical twin Eva Kor at
a Washington, D.C. gathering of Holocaust survivors. Eva met fraternal
twin Marc Berkowitz at that event, and C.A.N.D.L.E.S. was born.

1.3. C.A.N.D.L.E.S. Memorial Candle. These candles would be placed in six locations at Auschwitz, to recognize the six million Jews who perished in the camps across Europe; four million people died at Auschwitz.

1.4. C.A.N.D.L.E.S. banner: "Eternity: Auschwitz Twins." This banner was displayed at all significant activities conducted by C.A.N.D.L.E.S.

2. Pre-Event Activities: Meeting Twins

In December 1984, several weeks before leaving for Poland, I was invited to a gathering at the home of René (Guttmann) Slotkin, located on New York City's upper west side. René had survived Auschwitz-Birkenau along with his twin sister, Irene Hizme (née Renate Guttmann). The twins were just six years old when they arrived at the camp in December 1943 and were placed in separate barracks; they didn't meet again until they were twelve and a half years old. A Long Island, NY couple had adopted Irene—and when she told her new parents she had a twin brother, they found him in Czechoslovakia and brought him to the United States to be with his sister. The extraordinary twist of events leading to their reunion is told in their 2005 film, *Rene and I: From Auschwitz to America*;[7] also see additional annotation for photograph 6.6.

Other people present at this gathering were Peter Somogyi, a fraternal twin who had spent time at Auschwitz-Birkenau and his wife Anna, as well as the twins' spouses, June Slotkin and Samuel (Sam) Hizme. Interestingly, June has an identical twin sister, Jean, and Sam had a fraternal twin sister, Shirley, now deceased. A reporter from a local Jewish newspaper was also present.

Intriguing events occurred as we sat around the Slotkins' large dining room table. Two moments are memorable. Peter, who was eleven years old when he entered Auschwitz-Birkenau with his twin brother Tom (Tomas), picked up a pencil and sketched a map of the camp on a sheet of white paper. His wife, Anna, was stunned because in all their years of marriage Peter had rarely spoken to her or to his children about this experience. I discreetly picked up that little map, placed it in my notebook and kept it for many years. The other event that has remained with me is Irene's sudden statement that "Mengele wore green boots!" She announced this with great certainty after denying that she had many memories from the camp. Psychologists studying

---

7   G. M. Angelone, Director (2005). *Rene and I: From Auschwitz to America* (New York: Twin Pix Production, LLC).

traumatized individuals believe that their memories can return when their experiences are validated and receive emotional support.[8]

One of my missions during the visit to Auschwitz would be to determine the actual identity number (IDNO) that had been tattooed into René's arm when he arrived at Auschwitz-Birkenau. His number (169061) is a string of 0s, 1s, 6s, and 9s, so can be read differently depending on which way he holds his arm. Having this personal information was important to him. Interestingly, the opposite-sex twin pairs did not appear to have contiguous IDNOS

2.1. René Slotkin (Guttmann) (left (L) and Irene Hizme (Guttmann) (1985) at age forty-seven years. The twins were featured in the 2005 film, *Rene and I: From Auschwitz to America*. Irene passed away in May 2019, at age 81; René passed away in July 2022, at age 84, as this book was going into production. René preferred using the accent mark in his name, but interestingly it does not appear in the film's title.

8   David Hosier, "Childhood Trauma and Memory—Why Some Remember, Others Forget." *Childhoodtraumarecovery.com*, https://childhoodtraumarecovery.com/all-articles/childhood-trauma-and-memory-why-some-remember-others-forget/, accessed 2022.

as did the same-sex twins—Irene's number was 70917.[9] René and Irene would not be visiting Auschwitz-Birkenau, but I would meet them again in Israel for the public hearing at Yad Vashem. René explained that he and Irene did not feel terribly affected by having been in the camp. Curious, I asked him why he had held this particular gathering at his home, and why he would be traveling to Israel. He answered, "Because I thought there might be something in it for me."

2.2. Fraternal twins, Tom Simon (Tomas) Somogyi (L) and Peter (Péter) Somogyi, originally from Pécs, Hungary. Tom and his wife Lisa now live in Ontario, Canada; Peter and his wife Anna now live in Wilmington, Delaware. This photograph was taken in Jerusalem, 1985. A photograph of Peter and Tom Somogyi, taken in March 1945 after their return to Pécs following the January 1945 liberation of Auschwitz, hangs in the rabbi's office of the original synagogue in Pécs; also see photograph 10.13.

9   C.A.N.D.L.E.S., "Mengele Twins Found by CANDLES." C.A.N.D.L.E.S. Holocaust Museum and Education Center, https://candlesholocaustmuseum.org/educational-resources/twins-found-by-candles.html, 2022.

3. Traveling to Poland

January 24. Travel to Poland with the twins and their companions began at TWA's terminal at John F. Kennedy airport. The first part of the journey took us from New York City to Paris (Orly Airport) where we boarded a train for the city; we would fly to Warsaw later that night. This brief excursion was an opportunity to meet the members of our unique travel group that included twin and non-twin survivors, their children, members of the public, and members of the press.[10] I was amazed to discover Auschwitz survivor Mike Vogel, from Indiana, whose daughter Caryn had worked with me at the Illinois State Psychiatric Institute during my graduate student years. In fact, I had met Mike at Caryn's wedding. I also met *Los Angeles Times* reporters Bob Dallos and Ron Soble, who were going to Poland to cover the twins' reunion, as well as the experiences of Polish citizens who had moved to the United States but returned home.

January 25. Later that evening, we boarded an Air Lot flight in Paris bound for Warsaw. The aisles (rather than the rows as in most other aircraft) were designated as "smoking" and "non-smoking" sections, exposing non-smokers to the smell and fumes they hoped to avoid. The restrooms were the largest I have ever seen on an airplane. I still have my copy of Air Lot's inflight magazine, *Kaleidoscope,* dated 2/21/84.

After landing in Warsaw, our group boarded a bus for the *Hotel Grand-Orbis—Warszawa* for the night. My guest card, which I discovered while writing this book, showed that my room assignment was 329. The hotel was modern and comfortable, but uninteresting and nondescript. I was grateful that my suitcase had arrived intact, protected by the bright yellow tag that had been fastened to its handle before we left New York; the tag was tucked inside my copy of *Kaleidoscope.*

There was little time for exploring Warsaw, but I recall the half-empty shelves of food shops and clothing stores. Knowing that I craved fruit, Andy Berkowitz (son of twin survivor Marc Berkowitz) presented me with some

---

10 Jon Shean, one of several correspondents working for CBS news, interviewed several of the twins.

apples he had found, albeit slightly spoiled. And I managed to buy a beautiful gray fur hat that I still love.

January 26. The next day we boarded another bus that would bring us to Krakow, approximately 225 miles to the south. We arrived at the *Holiday Inn Krakow*, where we would spend the next five nights. Joining us were several new twin survivors, family members and television news correspondents.[11] Buses transported us each day from Krakow to Auschwitz, about 45 miles away. Our first visit to Auschwitz-Birkenau would be the following day, January 27, 1985—exactly forty years to the day that the camp was liberated by Soviet forces.

3.1. Former United States Representative Elizabeth Holtzman with fraternal twin Marc Berkowitz. She came to wish us well as we were preparing to fly from New York City (John F. Kennedy Airport) to Paris before transferring to Warsaw. The date is January 24, 1985. *See Additional Annotation.*

3.1. Elizabeth Holtzman, a Democrat, represented New York's 16th congressional district for four consecutive terms (1973-1981). She also has a fraternal twin brother named Robert.* Marc Berkowitz, co-founder of C.A.N.D.L.E.S., had arrived at Auschwitz-Birkenau at age twelve. "After the war there was no childhood for the children of Auschwitz," he said.

* Eli Lederhendler, "Elizabeth Holtzman." Jewish Women's Archive, https://jwa. org/encyclopedia/article/holtzman-elizabeth, June 23, 2021.

---

11   Sadly, Bob Dallos passed away in August 1991; Ron Soble passed away in June 2021. We were in touch for a while after the twins' reunion, especially after Mengele's body was discovered in Embu, Brazil, in August 1985. I have fond memories of them both.

3.2. Preparing to leave JFK Airport for Paris, en route to Warsaw.
Several twin survivors brought their children with them. Andy Berkowitz,
son of Marc Berkowitz (R), is in the foreground.

3.3. Ron Soble,
one of two *Los Angeles
Times* reporters who
came to cover the trip.
He is seated on the train
that took us from
the airport in Paris
to the city.

4. Visiting Auschwitz-Birkenau: Reunion and Re-enactment

Our group spent four days (January 27–January 30) visiting Auschwitz-Birkenau. The bus ride from Krakow to Auschwitz-Birkenau took about 90 minutes, and every freezing cold day brought chilling reminders of what the twins had endured. Only eight twins and their family members and friends were able to attend (one of the twins stayed at the hotel due to an illness), but we were joined by over forty more at the Jerusalem hearing. There were, however, seventeen camera crews from the United States and Europe. Two members of the Israeli Parliament, Shevach Weiss and Dov Shilansky (a Dachau survivor), were also present.[12]

As we approached our destination it was possible to see the tracks over which trains transporting Jews and other prisoners traveled. At the station ramp Nazi officers called out for twins, who were taken to a special location, giving Dr. Mengele easy access to them for his cruel medical experiments. The twins were safer for a while, but their safety was fleeting.

Our first day was devoted mostly to hearing the twins recall their happy childhoods in Europe and the stark contrast with the frightening events awaiting them at Auschwitz-Birkenau. They reminded us that they were relatively young survivors whose history had been generally neglected by Holocaust scholars. Visiting the camp was also a rare opportunity for the twins to share their life histories with their children and, in a sense, visit the graves of their family members who had perished.

January 27, 1985, was an extraordinary day—the 40th anniversary of the liberation of the camp. The Nazi officers, anticipating the arrival of the Soviet army, tried to destroy evidence of their horrendous activities and move the prisoners to other locations. The exodus from Auschwitz came to be known

---

12 Michael T. Kaufman, "Auschwitz Echoes to Prayer as Mengele's Victims Return." *New York Times*, Section A, p. 1, 4, https://timesmachine.nytimes.com/timesmachine/1985/01/28/038741.html?pageNumber=4.

as the "death march" because many prisoners were too ill or too weak to withstand the physical exertion and the frigid January winter.

Our days were filled with visits to the twins' barracks, the ruins of a crematorium, a field where Nazi officers played soccer with the *sonderkommando* (elite prisoners whose skills were needed to keep the camp functioning), a monument to the four million people who perished at Auschwitz-Birkenau and other significant sites.[13] We searched the records for twins' names, dates and places, confirmation that several twins had requested to show they had truly been there. This was important—a female twin was unrecognized by the others, and several twins with medical problems hoped to learn more about the experimental procedures they had endured. Our nights together at dinner, coffee, and drinks were valuable and much needed opportunities to process the scenes and sights we had previously known only from books and films.

The pictures in this section are briefly annotated as in the previous sections to provide context and meaning—but the scenes speak for themselves. The C.A.N.D.L.E.S. Memorial Pledge that appears in photograph 4.8 is reproduced below. Plaques bearing these words were placed at the railroad platform at Auschwitz, the gas chamber in Birkenau, and the ovens in Auschwitz. A plaque was also left at Yad Vashem in Jerusalem (*C.A.N.D.L.E.S. Newsletter*, Spring 1985). The gorgeous calligraphy seen in the pledge, as well as in the banners and candles, was done by Irene Hizme, twin survivor of Auschwitz-Birkenau.

C.A.N.D.L.E.S. Memorial Pledge

We, C.A.N.D.L.E.S., are the voices of the children
saved from the ashes. We pledge to do the following:

We will not let the world forget what happened here in Auschwitz.

We will remember that a part of humanity perished here.
This soil is soaked with the blood, the tears,
and the ashes of our mothers and fathers, sisters and brothers.

---

13 Auschwitz-Birkenau State Museum, "Memorial and Museum: International Monument." http://www.auschwitz.org/en/gallery/memorial/international-monument/, 2022.

*We will show our children
where their grandparents hugged us for the very last time.*

*We will work together to eliminate prejudice
from the face of the earth.*

We will not rest until Dr. Josef Mengele is caught and brought to justice.

*We will appeal to the conscience of the world
never to let this happen again.*

January 27, 1985

4.1. Train tracks to Auschwitz Birkenau, from our bus window,
January 27, 1985.

4.2. Approach to the Auschwitz-Birkenau railroad ramp.

4.3. Auschwitz-Birkenau from the Tower.

4.4. Entrance to Birkenau from Auschwitz.

4.5. Wooden Barracks of Birkenau.

4.6. The Barracks of Birkenau, Day 1, January 27, 1985.

4.7. Auschwitz: Kaduk's Chapel, named after the brutal SS officer Oswald Kaduk, is in the background. I was told that Nazi officers stayed there during roll call while prisoners stood outside in the cold. *See Additional Annotation.*

4.7. SS officers were part of the *Schutzstaffel* ("protective Echelon"), the organization responsible for guarding Adolf Hitler. It became a highly feared body as its functions widened.

Kaduk's Chapel is located between the barracks and main camp of Auschwitz. "Oswald Kaduk." https://military-history.fandom.com/wiki/Oswald_Kaduk#:~:text=Kaduk%20is%20also%20known%20for%20Kaduk%27s%20chapel%2C%20a,worked%20in%20a%20sugar%20factory%20in%20L%C3%B6bau, accessed July 2022; Editors, "The SS." https://www.history.com/topics/world-war-ii/ss, June 7, 2019

4.8. Identical twins, Eva Kor (L) & Miriam Czaigher,
placing the C.A.N.D.L.E.S. memorial pledge and wreath at Auschwitz.
The yellow stars were worn to recall that Jews living in countries controlled
by the Reich were required to wear them for identification.
January 27, 1985.

4.9. Eva Kor leading the group of twins and family members
on our first day at Auschwitz-Birkenau—her aim was to encourage twins
to remember what happened years ago. To the right of the photograph
is Eva's son Alex; to the left of the photograph are Ephraim Reichenberg
(whose story comes later) and Eva's daughter, Rina.

4.10. Gathering of twins and a twin's child for song and prayer.

4.11. Candles and a wreath placed at the ruins of a crematorium,
destroyed by a group of *Sonderkommando* (elite prisoners).

4.12. Once electrified barbed wire. The sign reads: Warning, High Voltage, Risk of Death.

4.13. Eva Kor placed her hand on the once electrified barbed wire.

4.14. Menashe Lorenczy,
fraternal opposite-sex twin,
in prayer.

4.15. Fraternal twin, Vera
Kriegel, lifted her sleeve
to show us her tattooed
identity number: A-26946.

4.16. Twin survivor Vera Kriegel is in the center. She is standing next to Israeli Parliament members Shivach Weiss (L) and Dov Shilansky (R).

4.17. Yona (Fux) Laks, identical twin. She is in the twins' barracks, lifting her sleeve to reveal the number tattooed into her arm upon arrival in the camp: A-27700.

4.18. Yona (Fux) Laks and twin sister Miriam Fux– after liberation.

4.19. Sketch of twins: could they be Yona and Miriam?
See Additional Annotation.

4.19. I photographed this sketch of a pair of identical twins I found in the archives maintained at Auschwitz-Birkenau. I wondered if this rendering was of the twins Yona and Miriam. Note the white blotch on the lower left area of the photograph. When I was bringing my used film through the airport in Poland (en route to Paris and Jerusalem), I was careful to place it in protective lead bags. However, I forgot that I had left a partly used roll of film in my camera. I pleaded with the officer in charge to allow me to hand carry it through the gate, but he refused. The same white blotch appears in about ten to fifteen of my photographs.

4.20. Fraternal twin, Vera Kriegel, holds a banner in preparation
for a reenactment of the death march that took place on January 27, 1945.
This photograph was taken exactly forty years after the actual event.
J'accuse (French) means "I accuse;" the Hebrew phrase under the star
translates as, "Forever Twins of Auschwitz."

4.22. The International Monument to the Victims of Fascism at Auschwitz-Birkenau was dedicated in 1967. It has commemorative plaques in twenty-two languages. The monument can be viewed at https://www.auschwitz.org/en/gallery/memorial/international-monument/==al.

◀ 4.21. Liberation of Auschwitz/death march reenactment. *J'accuse* is the branch of C.A.N.D.L.E.S. formed by the Israeli twins. The gentleman in the tan coat is Mike Vogel, a non-twin-survivor and father of my friend Caryn whom I referenced in the Introduction to this section. January 27, 1945/1985. Israeli Parliament member Shevach Weiss is behind him. Identical twins Eva Kor (L) and Miriam Czaigher are in the middle of the picture in blue. Grasping her mother's arm is Miriam's daughter Angela Czaigher. Identical twin Yona Lux is on the far right and behind her is Israeli Parliament member Dov Shilansky. Fraternal twin Marc Berkowitz, who is wearing a black cap, is behind Shevach Weiss and Eva Kor.

5. Exploring Auschwitz-Birkenau: An Art Museum, a Chance Meeting, and a Trip to the Polish Border

Our days at Auschwitz-Birkenau gave us lots of time for exploring the exhibits, files, and photographs that are available for public viewing. On our second day at the camp, January 28, I learned that there was an art museum at Auschwitz, and I left the group to explore it on my own. The museum displays paintings, sketches and statues created by both artists and former prisoners who had survived and established new lives. These works of art depict details of the death camp experience, some probably unknown.[14]

Exiting the museum, I caught sight of the late Holocaust survivor and scholar Elie Wiesel. Wiesel was visiting Auschwitz for the first time since his 1945 liberation, accompanied by the late *ABC* news anchor Peter Jennings. I wondered if Jennings had heard about the twins' reunion from his niece, whom I had met several months earlier during a Caribbean vacation—I remembered telling her about my plans to attend the C.A.N.D.L.E.S. reunion.[15]

There are some interesting back stories to my chance meeting with Wiesel. The photograph I took of him is the one exception in this collection in which a picture does not speak entirely for itself.

Knowing that Wiesel taught courses in Jewish studies at Boston University, I could have easily sent the photograph to him there, but I had hoped

---

14   The museum houses approximately 4,100 pieces of art of which half were created by prisoners. Auschwitz-Birkenau State Museum, "Memorial and Museum." http://www.auschwitz.org/en/museum/historical-collection/, 2022.

15   A brief filmed segment featuring Elie Wiesel's interview with Peter Jennings, "Elie Wiesel Returns to Auschwitz," was produced by *ABC News*. It can be viewed at https://abcnews.go.com/International/video/jan-28-1985-elie-wiesel-returns-auschwitz-68153496, January 28, 1985.

to present it to him personally.[16] An opportunity arose several years later when he delivered a talk at Orchestra Hall in Minneapolis, Minnesota, where I lived and worked at the time. I attended Wiesel's lecture and gave the picture to an usher who agreed to give it to him. Then, miraculously, as I was heading toward the bus stop on my way home, I noticed Wiesel walking alone, just ahead of me. I approached him, explained who I was and asked him if he had been given the picture. He smiled, said that he had received it and thanked me. I didn't expect to meet him again, but I did.

In February 2010, I was invited to attend former President Barack Obama's White House ceremony for the awarding of the National Medals in Arts and Humanities.[17] It turned out that Elie Wiesel was one of the awardees. As before, I went up to him and reminded him of who I was, and he nodded in recognition.

I did not spend our final day, January 30, at Auschwitz-Birkenau. Instead, I accompanied the *Los Angeles Times* reporters, Bob Dallos and Ron Soble, to Zakopane, a town in southern Poland at the foot of the Tatra Mountains, close to the Czech border. Dallos and Soble were writing the story of Polish citizens who had relocated to Chicago for financial reasons, then had unexpectedly returned to Poland. They had arranged for a driver (Chris) to bring us to the home of a couple who had gone through this experience. A required placard with the words "POLSKA AGENCJA INTERPRESS" was visible through our car window. Upon our return we dined at Wierzynek, an extraordinary restaurant that dates back to the mid-fourteenth century.[18]

---

16   Elie Wiesel was the Andrew W. Mellon Professor in Humanities and professor of philosophy and religion at Boston University, from 1976 to 2010. The Elie Wiesel Center for Jewish Studies was dedicated in 2005 and renamed in honor of his parents, Shlomoh and Sarah Wiesel. Elie Wiesel passed away on July 2, 2016. Judy Bolman-Fasman, "Remembering Elie Wiesel at Boston University." *Jewish Boston,* https://www.jewishboston.com/read/remembering-elie-wiesel-at-boston-university/, September 11, 2017; Elie Wiesel Center for Jewish Studies, "About us: Elie Wiesel Center for Jewish Studies." *BU Arts and Sciences,* https://www.bu.edu/jewishstudies/about/, accessed 2022.
17   The invitation to attend the White House event came from my friend and Minnesota state senator Richard J. Cohen. Senator Cohen was a member of the President's Committee on the Arts and Humanities, appointed by former President Barack Obama.
18   Robert E. Dallos, & Ron L. Soble, "Feasting as King in Fabulous Krakow Restaurant." *Los Angeles Times,* p. G28, June 9, 1985. The sumptuous meal cost the equivalent of $3 USD. Either Dallos or Soble offered to pay the bill in full.

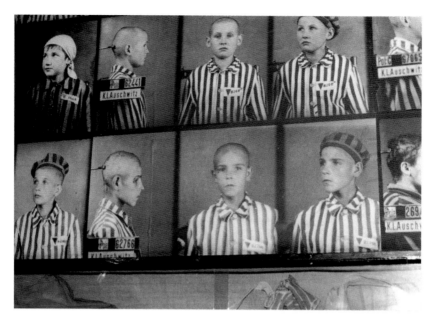

5.1. Twins were photographed and measured. Remnants of their clothing, taken upon arrival, are shown are below.

5.2. "Keep Calm." These words were written on a wall at Auschwitz-Birkenau.

5.3. Eva Kor (L) and Miriam Czaigher (Mozes) stand before their childhood images in film footage of the liberation by the Soviet army.

5.4. I photographed this picture of Miriam Czaigher (L) and Eva Kor, taken several years after their liberation as young girls.

5.5. Identical twin, Maurice (Morris) Frankovich, on January 28, 1985, in the twins' barracks, pointing to his childhood self in film footage of the Soviet liberation. His twin brother, Jacob, did not survive.

5.6. Fraternal twin, Marc Berkowitz, standing before his twelve-year-old image in film footage of the Soviet liberation.

5.7. I photographed this picture of fraternal twins, Vera Kriegel (L) and Olga Solomon (Grossman), and their family members.

5.8. I photographed these pictures of fraternal twins, Vera Kriegel (L) and Olga Solomon Grossman.

5.9. Eva Kor examining documents at Auschwitz-Birkenau. The notepad and pen on the table are mine.

3	7047-A	Kastner Iborla	23
4	7220-A	Sinje Klara	24
5	7221-A	Kemeński Magda	24
6	9750-A	Kemeński Klara	17
7	9749-A	Kerpel Ida	17
8	8736-A	Kerpel Mrta	43
9	8735-A	Kurz Edita	43
10	8740-A	Kurz Lilly	9
11	8739-A	Klein Anna	9
12	7213-A	Klein Judit	4
13	7214-A	Kohn Klara	4
14	5139-A	Kohn Ewa	19
16	5138-A	Keppes Teresa	19
17	7050-A	Keppes Ewa	15
18	7049-A	Labowicz Lilly	15
19	7051-A	Labowicz Ewa	21
20	7052-A	Lichtenstein Lilly 3632-A	21
51	3633-A	Lichtenstein Malvine	10
53	7059-A	Lörenzi Lea	10
54	12090-A	Lörenzi Andreas	2
55	5141-A	Lövinger Rosa	2
56	5142-A	Lövinger Helena	
57	5122-A	Lustig-Brauer Agnes	14
58	5121-A	Lustig-Brauer Ewa	14
59	5123-A	Lustig-Brauer Judit	14
70	7736-A	Malek Salomon	14
71	5131-A	Malek Judith	3
73	7737-A	Malek Elias	3
74	7738-A	Malek Jacob	11
75	3638-A	Mermelstein Valeria	11
76	3637-A	Mermelstein Marta	11
77	7064-A	Moses Miriam	11
78	7063-A	Moses Ewa	11
79	5750-A	Molnar Suse	20
80	5771-A	Molnar Marie	20
81	6034-A	Moszkowicz Rosa	18
82	6035-A	Moszkowicz Helena	18

5.10. This is a partial list of twins at Auschwitz-Birkenau, retrieved from the camp's archives. The names are arranged in alphabetical order, next to their identification numbers. Based on available dates of birth, the entries in the far-right column appear to be each twin's age at liberation. Some of these ages do not match those provided on the list of twins compiled by the C.A.N.D.L.E.S. Holocaust Museum; see https://candlesholocaustmuseum.org/educational-resources/twins-found-by-candles.html . It is possible that some young twins provided incorrect information, or that they or their parents claimed they were older than they were, believing this might spare them.

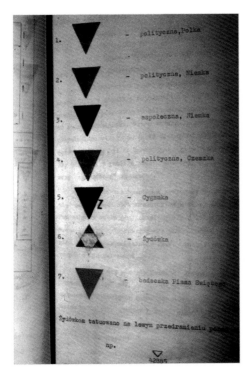

5.11. Symbols Worn
by Female Prisoners to Indicate
Their Classification.
From top to bottom:
1. Political prisoner (Polish),
2. Political prisoner (German),
3. Anti-Social (German,)
4. Political prisoner (Czech),
5. Gypsy,
6. Jew,
7. Scholar of the Holy Scriptures.
Source: Auschwitz Archives.

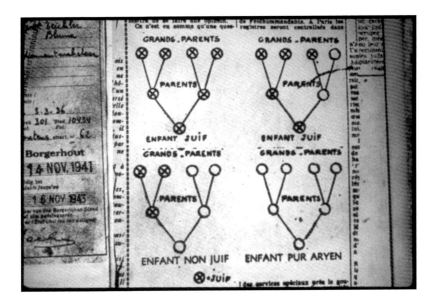

5.12. Genealogy charts defining who is a Jewish child. The extent to which this was applied is uncertain. Source: French Newspaper, Auschwitz-Birkenau.

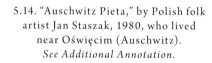

5.13. "Children," by Polish
artist Mieczyslaw Stobierski,
1950, from Krakow.
See Additional Annotation.

5.14. "Auschwitz Pieta," by Polish folk
artist Jan Staszak, 1980, who lived
near Oświęcim (Auschwitz).
See Additional Annotation.

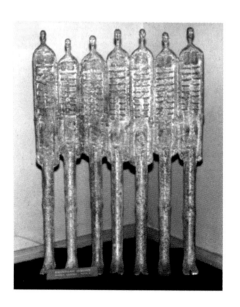

5.15. "Wall of Death," by Polish
artist Bronisław Chromy, 1962, from
Krakow. *See Additional Annotation.*

5.16. "Selection to the gas chamber," 1950, by former Auschwitz prisoner and survivor, Jerzy Potrzebowski. *See Additional Annotation.*

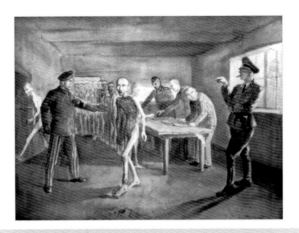

5.13—5.16. I took these photographs of the sculptures and painting at the Auschwitz-Birkenau State Museum.

Mieczyslaw Stobierski, the artist whose work is shown in photographs 5.12, was born in Sladów but moved to Krakow after the war. There he met his old friend, a former Auschwitz prisoner and painter, Tadeusz Myszkowski. That association caused Stobierski to create a series of sculptures depicting concentration camp themes. Geneaology.com, "Temple Family of Beaver County, PA: Information About Mieczyslaw Stobierski." https://www.genealogy.com/ftm/t/e/m/Fred-P-Temple/WEBSITE-0001/UHP-0220.html, 2022.

Jan Staszak lived in Kutno during the war, the location of a Jewish ghetto and transit camp that operated between 1940 and 1942. He met his future wife, Irena Mazgaj, a former slave laborer in the Monowitz sub-camp, while he engaged in postwar military service in Oświęcim (Auschwitz). They moved to Harmęże, near Brzezinka (Birkenau). Dr. Hab. Roma Sendyka, Dr. Erica Lehrer, Wojciech Wilczyk, & Magdalena Zych (Curators), "Terribly Close: Polish Vernacular Artists Face the Holocaust." http://www.terriblyclose.eu/exhibition/jan-staszak-gas/, 2019.

Bronisław Chromy was a painter, sculptor, draftsman and medalist, as well as a professor at the Academy of Fine Arts in Krakow. He is known for sculptures combining bronze and stone into a single form. He is responsible for many projects, including Pieta Oswiecimska (1963). "Facts About Bronisław Chromy." Askart, https://www.askart.com/artist/Bronislaw_Chromy/11183032/Bronislaw_Chromy.aspx, accessed 2022.

Jerzy Potrzebowski was born in Sandomierz, Poland and arrived in Auschwitz in 1943. As an artist and former prisoner, he became part of a team working on an exhibition for the State Museum of Oświęcim. The International Center for Education about Auschwitz and the Holocaust, and The Auschwitz-Birkenau State Museum, "The Auschwitz Experience in the Art of Prisoners: Jerzy Potrzebowski." https://www.vermilionadvantage.com/wp-content/uploads/2022/02/Auschwitz-Experience_v.Final-Print-2.pdf, accessed 2022.

5.17. Holocaust survivor and scholar, Elie Wiesel, on his first visit to Auschwitz-Birkenau. He was accompanied by the late Peter Jennings, *ABC News*. January 28, 1985.

5.18. Visiting Zakopane, Poland. This Polish gentleman (L) spent time in Chicago for financial reasons, but returned to Poland. I am standing on the right. Photo credit: Bob Dallos, reporter for the *Los Angeles Times*.

5.19. Scene from a town outside Zakopane, Poland. January 30, 1985.

5.20. Zakopane, Poland. I am on the left, standing next to *Los Angeles Times* reporter Bob Dallos. This photo was taken either by Ron Soble or the Polish gentleman they had interviewed.

5.21. I saved our car sign that reads:
Polska Agencja Interpress
(Polish Interpress Agency).
Press passes signify journalistic
legitimacy and offer access
to restricted areas. Poland was
under communist control in 1985
so it was important to indicate
our identity.

5.22. Our driver,
Chris, brought us from
Krakow to Zakopane
and was with us on the
return trip.

6. Medical Experiments: Process and Purpose

The classic twin study is a simple, elegant, and well-respected approach for disentangling genetic and environmental influences on human characteristics. The degree of similarity between identical twins (who share 100% of their genes) and fraternal twins (who share 50% of their genes, on average) is compared. Greater resemblance between identical twins than fraternal twins demonstrates genetic influence on the trait(s) under study. Establishing twin type is a crucial first step in any twin investigation, because misclassifying identical twins as fraternal, or fraternal twins as identical yields inaccurate and misleading results.[19]

The natural twinning rate in Caucasian populations is one in eighty births with identical twins comprising one-third of the pairs. The current twinning rate in western nations is approximately one in thirty-two births, owing to assisted reproductive technologies (ART) and older age at conception; older maternal age is linked to an increased chance of conceiving fraternal twins. ART was not discovered until 1978, so prior twin research was based on natural twinning rates.[20]

There are two competing theories as to why Mengele was so taken with twin studies. The first explanation is that he wished to unravel the biological bases of twinning and apply them to increase the German population. However, if that were the case, I believe Mengele would have focused more closely on the twins' parents, rather than the twins. The other explanation is that Mengele hoped to demonstrate the genetic superiority of the Aryan people, consistent with Nazi ideology. I believe this second view comes closer to capturing Mengele's intent. [21] However, the experiments he conducted would not seem to bring him any closer to answering either question.

---

19   Nancy L. Segal, *Entwined Lives: Twins and What They Tell Us About Human Behavior* (New York: Plume, 2000).

20   Nancy L. Segal, *Twin Mythconceptions: False Beliefs, Fables, and Facts About Twins* (New York: Elsevier, 2017).

21   Robert Jay Lifton (1982). "Medicalized Killing in Auschwitz." *Psychiatry* 45 (4): 283-297; *The Nazi Doctors: Medical Killing and the Psychology of Genocide* (New York: Basic Books, Inc., 1986).

The procedures used by Mengele were painful and cruel; some of his techniques will be described in Section 8. At the same time, he gathered information on the twins, such as height and eye color, that current researchers continue to collect. Thus, according to psychiatrist Robert Jay Lifton, "Mengele's dedication to the Nazi biomedical vision kept him always on the border between science and ideologically-corrupted pseudoscience, a border very important to understand."[22]. Measurements made on the twins are listed below, translated from a document I discovered at the Auschwitz archives:

Length of head	Width of shoulders (largest)
Width of head (smallest)	Width of shoulders (smallest)
Width of head	Length of arm
Distance across face	Length of forearm
Length of face	Length of hand
Length of nose	Width of hand
Width of nose	Length of leg
Color of eyes	Length of foot
Color of hair	Width of foot
Breast bone (depth)	Number of siblings
Length of spine	Paternal siblings (number)
Body height	Maternal siblings (number)

The information on body measurements gathered at Auschwitz-Birkenau is highly suspect, given the twins' unrepresentative physical conditions and emotional states. Furthermore, one of the twins (Frank Klein; *see section 8*) revealed to me that when asked about the number of paternal or maternal siblings in his family he simply made up a number—and the Nazi officer recorded it as fact.

Some measure of controversy surrounds the current and future use and usefulness of the twin data and other information obtained from prisoners of Auschwitz and other death camps.[23] I believe that the material gathered from

---

22   Robert Jay Lifton (1982), "Medicalized Killing in Auschwitz." *Psychiatry* 45 (4): 283-297 (p. 289)

23   Nancy L. Segal, "Twin Research at Auschwitz-Birkenau: Implications for the Use of Nazi Data Today," in *When Medicine Went Mad: Bioethics and the Holocaust*, ed. Arthur L. Caplan (Totowa, NJ: Humana Press, 1992), 281-99. Also see other contributions to this volume.

the twins should never be included in research because of the dangerous signal that would be sent to future investigators. This action would imply that it is possible to bypass standards for human research since such data *may* prove valuable at a later date.[24] However, it is difficult to imagine that the materials Mengele and his colleagues collected could be more useful now than data gathered by the more modern sophisticated methods that have met human subject standards.[25]

The panel concluded, as did I, that the experiments were devoid of scientific value. The procedures were cruel, brutal, and painful and, according to geneticist and panelist Arno Motulsky, went far beyond any form of inquiry that would allow for reasonable scientific interpretation.[26] Moreover, there is no evidence that Mengele organized the twins by twin type (identical or fraternal), a critical first step in any twin research pursuit, as I indicated; in fact, I am aware of at least four pairs who were either nontwin siblings or "pseudotwins"—unrelated individuals who were classified as twins by quick-thinking inmates—a designation that spared their lives, at least for a while. Finally, the experiments were performed on physically weak and emotionally fragile individuals whose state was hardly characteristic of the human condition.

Many of the twins' records have never been recovered. As they age, they battle various diseases and other conditions, some baffling to their physicians. For example, one doctor wondered how an educated woman living in an affluent Chicago suburb contracted tuberculosis. The twins' uncertainty surrounding the source of their current health problems—ordinary aging or death camp treatment—is another battle they must conquer.

24 Nancy L. Segal, *Deliberately Divided: Inside the Controversial Study of Twins and Triplets Adopted Apart* (New York: Rowman & Littlefield, 2021).

25 Robert Jay Lifton (1982). "Medicalized Killing in Auschwitz." *Psychiatry* 45 (4): 283-297; *The Nazi Doctors: Medical Killing and the Psychology of Genocide* (New York: Basic Books, Inc., 1986).

26 Detailed documentation of experiments performed on the twins is presented by a physician who observed many of them firsthand. Miklos Nyiszli, *Auschwitz: A Doctor's Eyewitness Account* (New York, Fawcett Crest, 1960).

6.1. Dr. Ella Lingens-Reiner was a Polish physician in the camp and Secretary of the Sigmund Freud Society, in Vienna, at the time of the public hearing at Yad Vashem. She attended the hearing at the request of Nazi hunter Simon Wisenthal. She knew of Mengele's experiments and said he worried that others would steal his twin data. Dr. Lingens-Reiner had been sent to Auschwitz because she and her husband helped Jewish people escape from Poland. She noted that as a non-Jew and a physician, she was in a privileged position in the camp. Her Auschwitz-Birkenau experience is documented in her book *Prisoners of Fear* (1948, Victor Gollancz Publisher) and was described at the public hearing.

6.2. This is one of several photographs that was spoiled when I was not allowed to hand carry a partly used roll of camera film when leaving Poland. I believed it was important to include it in this collection. This picture shows a list of victims whose anthropological measurements, such as height and head width, were meticulously recorded by the Nazi doctors.

6.3. "Fraternal twin" Ephraim Reichenberg, leading the group of twins, friends, and government officials in prayer on January 27, 1985, the first day of the twins' gathering at Auschwitz-Birkenau. He is holding a small device to his neck as he speaks, having lost his voice as a result of experiments at Auschwitz. *See Additional Annotation for his complete story.*

6.3. Ephraim was not a twin, but he was assigned as one by Nazi officers when he entered Auschwitz-Birkenau alongside his near-in-age older brother, Laslo, when they exited the train from Budapest. It was observed that Laslo had a beautiful singing voice, whereas Ephraim did not, so it was decided to see why "twins" might differ in this way. Ephraim suffered painful injections into his throat, leaving his vocal cords severely damaged. After an operation in Israel to remove his vocal cords, he was able to speak only with the assistance of his hand-held device, designed by a German manufacturer. His brother, Laslo, perished at Auschwitz.

6.4. Fraternal twin, Menashe Lorenzcy, in prayer on the first day of the Auschwitz-Birkenau gathering, January 27, 1985. Next to him is Israeli Parliament member Dov Shilanksy. Menashe saved his twin sister Leora's life by faking a toothache. *See Additional Annotation.*

6.5. I photographed this picture of fraternal opposite-sex twins, Leora (L) and Menashe, at age 5 or 6 years.

6.4. At age nine, Menashe Lorenczy was thinking beyond his years. He and another twin boy had been given the task of transporting soup from the kitchen to the twins' barracks. The boys used this opportunity to secure extra bits of food and supplies. Menashe decided that his twin sister, Leora, could hide in the empty soup container on the way to the kitchen and, once there, could find additional food items to eat. When the soup container was full and ready to be carried, Menashe instructed his sister to hold her hand on the lid to keep it from sliding off—a clever excuse in the event that they were questioned by an officer on the return trip.

On another occasion, Menashe saved Leora from the crematorium and certain death. Following an experimental operation in the hospital, Leora developed an infection. The children understood that virtually no one who entered the hospital ever left. Menashe faked a toothache to be admitted and while his healthy tooth was extracted, he managed to escape the hospital with his sister by joining a group of children that were returning to the barracks. See Nancy L. Segal (1985), "Holocaust Twins: Their Special Bond." *Psychology Today*, 19 (8): 52-58.

6.6. Renate (L) and René Guttmann and their mother, Ita (Aisenscharf), taken at Theresienstadt, the transit camp for Jewish people, in Czechoslovakia. The twins were later adopted at different times by the Slotkin family in Long Island, NY.
This photo is in the collection of the United States Holocaust Museum, courtesy of the twins.
See Additional Annotation.

6.6. Mother and twins remained in Theresienstadt for six months, prior to their relocation to Auschwitz where they were separated from one another. They were transported to the camps after the 1941 arrest of the twins' father, Herbert, by the Gestapo (secret German police). Herbert, who was not Jewish, belonged to a group aimed at avoiding the Nazi occupation; after his discovery and imprisonment he was sent to Auschwitz and shot to death.

As told to me by René's widow June, René exited the camp on a death march between Birkenau and Auschwitz I (the main camp) during the Russian liberation. (Other twin boys were escorted out of the camp by Zvi Spiegel; I tell Spiegel's story in section 8 of this book.) The Russians and the Red Cross treated survivors in the infirmary of Auschwitz I. From there, René was sent to a hospital-sanatorium in the Carpathian Mountains to cure his tuberculosis where he was cared for by nursing nuns. A Czech physician, Dr. Kalina, was the head doctor and soon took René into his home in Košice; René was cured of the disease after several months of treatment. It turned out that Dr. Kalina, who had been raising René, had to flee his country for Palestine due to his political activities when the Communists came into power. He left René in the care of his sister.

Irene was taken from Birkenau (Auschwitz II) by a Polish Catholic woman whose home was in Oświęcim, the town adjacent to Birkenau. She was later found by the Czech Rabbi Forhand who searched for Jewish children taken into Christian homes. After a short stay in a Jewish-run home, Irene was transferred to a Jewish orphanage in Foublaines, outside of Paris, that had been established for World War II orphans. Irene was the only child there who had been in a concentration camp; many other children had been in hiding during the war. Her next visit was to New York City—*Rescue Children, Inc.* had arranged a special excursion for Irene and a young Jewish boy from a different orphanage, during which they enjoyed treats, toys, and celebrity meetings. This event was described in *Life Magazine,* in the November 17, 1947 issue. Irene had hoped to return to the French orphanage where she had formed meaningful friendships, but that was not to be. Instead, she was adopted at age nine by a Long Island couple, Dinah and Meyer Slotkin, who had a daughter, Debby, but were unable to conceive additional children. Irene asked the family to locate her twin brother. Interestingly, Dr. Kalina played a crucial role in the quest to find René—Kalina was living in the city of Haifa when he discovered the *Life Magazine* article about Irene's trip to New York and realized she was René's twin sister.

René, who had no official papers or documents, was eventually brought to the United States with the help of high-level United States government officials, including then U.S. President Harry S. Truman. Meyer Slotkin used a political connection to meet with President Truman in the Oval Office, and persuaded him to lift the restriction on the number immigrants allowed to enter the United States.*

Irene recalled the twins' reunion clearly. At age twelve years she stood taller than her twin brother, having gone through her adolescent growth spurt ahead of him, which is characteristic of adolescent females. And at the time they did not speak the same language. When they saw each other again for the first time they found themselves "at a loss for words," but not just because of the language barrier. "It was anticlimactic," she told me when I spoke with her in December 2021. "But I knew it was my brother."

---

* June Slotkin (widow of René Slotkin), Interview with Nancy L. Segal, 2022.

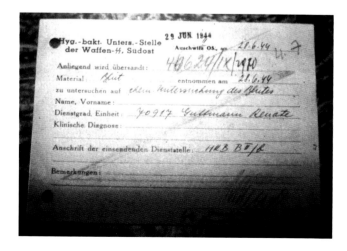

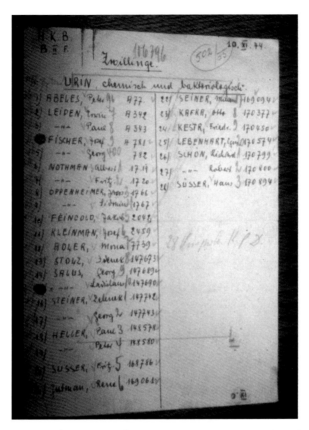

6.8. René Guttmann (later Slotkin) is number 21 on this list. The title is: Twins: Urine, Chemistry and Bacteriology. Presumably, the twins' blood samples would be tested for various elements. Before I left for Auschwitz-Birkenau, René asked me to verify his tattooed identity number (*see Section 2*).

◀ 6.7. Mengele's request for a blood sample from twin Renate Guttmann (later named Irene Hizme). The blood sample was taken on June 21, 1944, from this little girl who had been forcibly separated from her mother and her twin brother, René.
The specimen was to be studied at station HRB BII/b; the document bears the stamped signature of SS-Hauptsturmführer (Captain) Mengele.

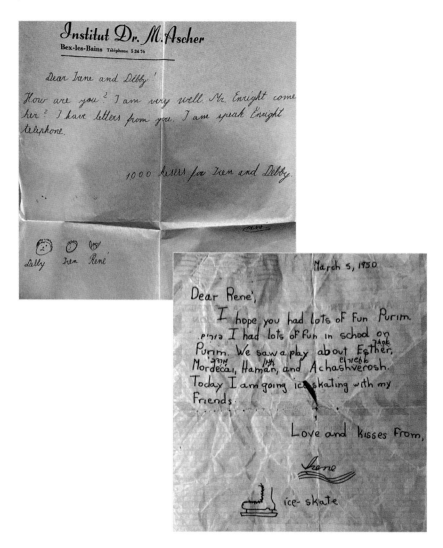

6.9. (Left) René Guttmann wrote this letter when he was still in Europe,
while his adoption by Meyer and Dinah Slotkin was moving forward.
The letter was sent to his twin sister, Irene, and to the Slotkins' daughter,
Debby, who would become his sister.
The twins were reunited on March 29, 1950, when they were 12 years old.

(Right) Irene sent letters to her brother like the one reproduced here.
Given the date of March 5, it is likely that this was the last letter that passed
between them before René came to the United States. A portion of this letter
is visible in the film, *Rene and I*. Both letters were made available
by Robin Hizme, Irene's daughter.
Note: Debby (Slotkin) Horowitz passed away on May 29, 2022.

6.10. Elizabeth and Perla (Ovici) were part of the Lilliput Troupe—entertainers from Hungary. These non-twin sisters were members of a family that included seven dwarfed children and several average sized children. At Auschwitz they were placed in a separate barracks for study. Upon seeing them, Mengele supposedly clasped his hands and announced that he had enough work to keep him busy for 20 years. The dwarfed siblings had to perform live for the Nazi officers; their teeth and feces were also examined. *See Additional Annotation.*

6.11. The Lilliput Troupe shown here was known for their singing and for playing music on small instruments. *See Additional Annotation.*

6.10–6.11. There were ten children in the Ovici family, seven of whom were dwarfed. I photographed two of the sisters at Yad Vashem (6.10) and a picture showing the seven members of the Lilliput Troupe (6.11). I questioned panelist and medical geneticist Dr. Arno Motulsky about the genetic underpinnings of their condition. He was uncertain—he thought one parent was affected, although one of the sisters had told him her parents were short, but within the range of normal human stature. A document published by *Cultural Heritage Through Image* indicates that the mother was "average sized," while the father was affected with dwarfism.*

* Jewish Heritage Foundation "Disability and the Holocaust: A History Revealed." *Cultural Heritage Through Image.* https://culturalheritagethroughimage.omeka.net/exhibits/show/disability/item/104, 2019.

6.12. Annetta Able (L) and Stephanie (Stepha) Heller (Heilbrunn) from Melbourne, Australia were originally from Subotica, Yugoslavia before moving to Prague, Czechoslovakia at age 3 years. They were scheduled to be part of an experiment to see if they would conceive twins if impregnated by twins. The experiment did not take place, due to the liberation. *See Additional Annotation.*

6.12. In 2015, at age ninety, Annetta Able and Stepha Heller were recognized as the oldest living twin survivors of Mengele's experiments.[*] Since her sister's passing in 2019, at age 95, Annetta, at age 98, is the oldest living twin survivor.

[*] Guinness World Records: Nancy L. Segal's contributor to Twins Page (2015). "Oldest twin Holocaust survivors." p. 63. *Guinness World Records.* London: Guinness World Records (Vancouver: Jim Pattison Group).

7. Touring Warsaw: War Memorials and Everyday Life

We left Krakow on January 31, on a bus bound for Warsaw where we would later board a plane to Paris, then Tel Aviv. This schedule allowed several hours for wandering through Warsaw's old sections and rebuilt areas, for visiting war memorials, palaces, and squares. These sites were variously painful, meaningful, surprising, and gratifying because of what we had experienced over the last four days at Auschwitz-Birkenau. It was painful seeing the Warsaw Ghetto monument, a tribute to the men and women who, in 1943, acted in resistance to the German occupiers of their country. Yet, it meant a great deal to see the restored sections of the city, evidence of the will to rebuild and the courage to recall.

I spent most of this day with twins Eva Kor and Marc Berkowitz, and with *LA Times* reporter Ron Soble. Toward afternoon, I was captivated by a surprising sight on the second-floor terrace of an apartment building (see photograph 7.9). An oversized sculpture of a human hand peeked out from above the railing, visible to all passersby. The depiction was a left hand, a curious feature since left-handedness occurs among a minority of most populations and is discouraged by some. The open palm seemed welcoming, but the intent of the owner or artist remains a mystery.

Proceeding through the airport customs, we did not know what airline (Air Lot or Air France) would transport us from Warsaw to Paris. This time we flew Air France. As we reached cruising height there was a wonderful moment during which two male survivors met after being separated for many years—most likely not knowing the fate of the other—and embraced each other warmly. Witnessing this happy commotion in the aisle as the two stared at each other in disbelief was heartening and gratifying. I do not recall who they were, but the memory of their extraordinary reunion has stayed with me. I would see other extraordinary events at the three-day hearing on Mengele's war crimes, at Yad Vashem, to begin on February 4, with social and educational events held on February 3.

7.1. Street leading to the Old Square in front of the King's Palace, in Warsaw.

7.2. Old Town (Stare Miasto), Market Square, Warsaw.

7.3. Castle Square (Plac Zamkowy) with the Royal Castle (Zamek Królewski) to the far right. This area of Warsaw was rebuilt after World War II.

7.4. *The Last March*, in the Warsaw Ghetto Square.
This photograph was actually taken in February 1985, at the Wall of Remembrance, Yad Vashem Holocaust Memorial, Jerusalem, Israel. The sculpture, created by Nathan Rapoport, was installed in 1976.

7.5. The Warsaw Ghetto Monument
(*Pomnik Bohaterów Getta*) at a distance.

7.6. Warsaw Ghetto Monument,
commemorating the heroes of the 1943 uprising.
The monument was designed by Nathan Rapoport.
Centered are twins Eva Kor (L) and Marc Berkowitz;
Los Angeles Times reporter Ron Soble is to the left.

7.7.–7.8. Warsaw Ghetto Memorial.

7.9. Warsaw—a friendly terrace.

7.10. Dr. Nancy L. Segal, Warsaw. I am wearing the fur hat I purchased in Warsaw at the start of the trip.

8. Twin Testimonies: Public Hearing on Josef Mengele's War Crimes

(February 3–6, 1985)

After our plane landed in Tel Aviv, we traveled to Jerusalem, arriving two days before the start of the public hearing. We stayed at the Holy Land Hotel, a venue offering gorgeous panoramic views of the Old City. Each day for the next four days, buses brought us to Yad Vashem, where the testimonies would take place, beginning February 4.

Opening events on February 3 included speeches by distinguished guests; the unveiling of the monument "Auschwitz" by Elza Pollack and dedication by Simone Veil; musical performances by the Tzahal quartet (Greek Holocaust survivors), identical twins (cellist and violinist) and conservatory choir (Musical Academy); and a dinner during which twins shared more of their unique life stories with one another.

Over the course of the next few days, we heard recollections and reflections from thirty survivors, mostly twins. The Hashmonaim Hall at Yad Vashem was filled with friends, family members, scholars, members of the media and concerned citizens. Several pairs of twins who had not been at Auschwitz-Birkenau were in the audience. Excitement and interest were palpable—everyone was highly motivated to find Mengele and bring him to justice, so documenting the twins' experiences was a critical step in this process. The best intelligence at that time placed Mengele in Paraguay under the protection of then President Alfredo Stroessner, but that later proved to be wrong.

The pictures I have selected for this section convey tragedy and heartbreak, but also courage and strength. Key features of the twins' testimonies are presented alongside many of the photographs, but in certain cases I have provided additional annotation, based on my interviews and notes. A more complete compilation of these testimonies is available in the journal *War Crimes*,

Genocide, and Crimes Against Humanity.[27] However, audience response to the testimonies of two survivors must be told.

Twenty-nine-year-old twin Zvi Spiegel was put in charge of forty or fifty twin boys whom he had to make available for experimentation when commanded to do so. Meanwhile, "Uncle Spiegel" made certain that the boys knew each other's names and he even taught them a little geography and mathematics when he could. On the day of liberation (January 27, 1945), he escorted thirty-six of his charges out of Auschwitz-Birkenau, leading them to their hometowns in Poland and Czechoslovakia; and did the same for other homeless children whom they met along the way. At the conclusion of Spiegel's testimony one of the panelists asked if any of the "twin boys" was in the audience and, if so, asked them to stand. There were eight. The applause lasted a long time—a very long time.[28,29]

Ruth Elias was the final survivor to testify. Ruth was not a twin—she was transported from her home in Czechoslovakia to Theresienstadt where she married and conceived a child. Three months pregnant when she arrived at Auschwitz, Ruth tried hard to conceal her condition, but eventually it was discovered; she delivered her baby daughter in the barracks of Auschwitz. Mengele ordered Ruth's breasts to be bandaged so she would be unable to feed the child—he did this ostensibly because he wanted to know how long an infant could survive without food. Of course, the baby grew weaker over the next few days—until Mengele informed Ruth that "tomorrow" he would come for them both. Knowing that mother and infant would be killed if she did not intervene, a Jewish prisoner-doctor handed Ruth a syringe filled with morphine, saying that her job was to save lives and that the baby had little chance of surviving. What happened next was hard to hear—Ruth Elias told

---

27   Grodin, M. A., Kor, E., & Benedict, S. (2011). "The trial that never happened: Josef Mengele and the twins of Auschwitz." *War Crimes, Genocide, and Crimes Against Humanity*, 5 (1 & 2), 3-90.

28   More about Zvi Spiegel can be found in Yoav Heller (2013), *The History of Zvi Spiegel: The Experience of Mengele Twins and Their Protector During the Holocaust and Its Aftermath* (Unpublished doctoral dissertation). Department of History, Royal Holloway, University of London. According to Heller, Spiegel eventually left the group at the railway station in Csap (Chop), located at the junction of Hungary, Czechoslovakia and what is present-day Ukraine, asking that the older twins lead the younger twins to their homes.

29   I met Yoav Heller in London, in 2011, when he was attending graduate school and I was attending a conference. He had contacted me upon learning from several of the surviving twins that I had attended the Yad Vashem hearing. Re-reading our email exchange from that time was enlightening.

us that she put her own daughter to death. The silence in the auditorium lasted for a long time—a very long time.[30]

At the conclusion of the public hearing the panel issued a resolution. I quote what I consider to be the two most important passages:

"There exists a body of evidence justifying the committal for trial of the S.S. physician Hauptsturmfuehrer Josef Mengele, for war crimes and crimes against humanity, including crimes against the Jewish people and against members of other nations."

"The commission also calls upon members of all nations to remember and to commemorate the catastrophe that Nazism wrought upon Europe and the Jewish people in particular, so that nowhere in the world may a regime rise which would perpetrate such horrible crimes upon members of any nation or upon any human being."

A final dinner was held at the Holy Land Hotel that evening for twin and nontwin survivors, family members, panelists, and guests. All of us would be leaving the next day, returning home, visiting with relatives, or touring the country. We were all changed in some way by the people we met and the stories we heard—but we shared the goals of finding Dr. Mengele and having him stand trial. Then unforeseen events intervened.

In June 1985, less than six months after the hearing ended, newspapers reported that the infamous Auschwitz physician was dead.[31] His death was attributed to a drowning accident in February 1979, in the south of Brazil where he had been living. The scientists involved in the investigation were convinced by the forensic evidence, but many twins were skeptical. A C.A.N.D.L.E.S. inquest, organized by twin survivor Eva Kor, took place in November 1985 in her hometown of Terre Haute, Indiana. The inquest is discussed in the following section.

---

30 More about Ruth Elias can be found in her book, *Triumph of Hope: From Theresienstadt and Auschwitz to Israel* (New York, Wiley, 1991)

31 William R. Long, "Brazil Body Mengele's, Forensic Scientists Say: Medical Findings and Other Evidence Called Overwhelming Proof of Nazi Doctor's Identity." *Los Angeles Times*, June 22, 1985, https://www.latimes.com/archives/la-xpm-1985-06-22-mn-2058-story.html

8.1. Public hearing: Mengele's war crimes, Yad Vashem.
The three days of testimony were February 4-6, 1985.

8.2. Model of the Holy Land Hotel, Jerusalem, Israel.

8.3. View from the Holy Land Hotel (model), Jerusalem, Israel.

8.4. Violin and cello performance by identical twins, Hillel and Nitai Tzur. Holy Land Hotel, February 3, 1985 (day before the first session of twins' testimonies). Eva Kor (L) and her identical twin sister, Miriam Czaigher, are seated to the left.

8.5. Unveiling and dedication of the monument "Auschwitz," by artist Elza Pollack. Standing at the microphone is Auschwitz survivor, Simone Veil (center), who was also the former Health Minister of France and first female President of the European Parliament, Yad Vashem, February 3, 1985.

8.6. Panel (public hearing on Mengele's experiments): Rafael Eitan (L), Yehuda Bauer, Gideon Hausner.

8.7. Panel members: Telford Taylor (L) and Arno Motulsky.

8.8. Panel members: Arno Motulsky and Simon Wisenthal; Zvi Terlo is missing but appears in the next photograph (8.9).

8.9. Full Panel (L to R): Rafael Eitan, Yehuda Bauer, Telford Taylor,
Simon Wiesenthal, Arno Motulsky, Zvi Terlo.
Testimony from Dr. Azriel Neeman (far L).
See Additional Annotations.

8.9. Full Panel, public hearing on Mengele's war crimes:
Rafi Eitan: Former advisor, Israeli government on terrorism.
Yehuda Bauer: Professor of History, Hebrew University, Jerusalem.
Gideon Hausner: Chairman of the Panel; Chief Prosecutor at the trial
   of Adolf Eichmann.
Telford Taylor: Prosecutor, Nuremburg Trials.
Arno Motulsky: Geneticist, University of Washington, Seattle.
Simon Wisenthal: Director of the Documentation Center of the Association
   of Jewish Victims of the Nazi Regime, Vienna.
Tvi Terlo: Attorney; Former Head, Israeli Ministry of Justice.
Dr. Azriel Neeman was a dentist at Auschwitz. He was aware of Mengele's
   experiments on twins and his interest in unusual genetic conditions.
   For example, Mengele was fascinated by a man who had six fingers
   (polydactyly). He had hoped to study him and was furious when he learned
   that the man had died.

8.10. Audience, public hearing, February 4, 1985.

8.11. Fraternal twin, Zvi Spiegel.
See Additional Annotation.

8.11. Zvi Spiegel saved the lives of two boys by giving them the same birthdate, thereby "assigning" them as twins. His twin sister, Magda, was placed in the barracks with the dwarfed performers; see photographs 6.10–6.11. Consequently, the young girls did not benefit from having an older twin in charge, as did the young boys. Regardless, given her devastation at losing her son, she would have been emotionally unable to have served in this role. Spiegel led the young male twins out of the camp after liberation, helping them reach their homes in Poland, Hungary, Czechoslovakia and other locations. He was 29 years old at the time.

8.12. Fraternal twin, Zvi Spiegel, testifying at the public hearing.
See Additional Annotation.

8.12. Spiegel testified that he once glanced at Dr. Mengele's notes and saw a questionnaire from the Kaiser-Wilhelm Institute, directed by Mengele's collaborator, Dr. Otmar Freiherr von Vershuer. According to Spiegel, the form was used to record and to compare hair color and various other physical characteristics, such as eye color and shape, and height from "top of the head to the toe."

8.13. Spiegel's list of young male twins he led to their hometowns after liberation. I photographed the list which is on display at Yad Vashem.

8.14. Zvi Spiegel (L) and fraternal twin Peter Somogyi. Spiegel helped Peter reach his home country of Hungary, along with Peter's twin brother, Tom, and other young boys.

8.15. Ephraim Reichenberg testifying at the Yad Vashem hearing. Note the hand-held device that allows him to speak. His vocal cords were severely damaged at Auschwitz-Birkenau as part of Mengele's experiments; see Section 6 and photograph 6.3.

8.16. Identical twins, Otto (L) and Frank Klein. *See Additional Annotation.*

8.16. Frank Klein (R) was on dialysis, yet felt compelled to attend the reunion and hearing. He brought his medical equipment and nurse with him. In section 6 (Medical Experiments), I showed a listing of the physical measurements made on the Mengele twins. As indicated earlier, Frank was a young child and told me he provided made-up answers when questioned about these measures by the officers. When the hearing ended some twins tried to arrange a kidney transplant for Frank, using the influence of the late Nancy Reagan, wife of former President Ronald Reagan; the Reagans lived in Texas where Frank was from. Sadly, Frank passed away during the operation.

8.17. Klein twins, parents, and sister Bella prior to entering Auschwitz-Birkenau.

8.18. Peter (Kleinmann) Greenfeld: Peter never found his twin sister, Miriam. *See Additional Annotation.*

8.18. Peter (Kleinmann) Greenfeld, originally from Czechoslovakia, was nicknamed "Pepicek" by the boys in his barracks. (Kleiner Peter means "Little Peter" in German.) After the liberation, Peter was found in the snow by a Mr. Greenfeld, who died three days later. Peter was raised by Greenfeld's daughter. He was sent to Auschwitz from Theresienstadt when he was three or four years old. Peter was told that his twin sister Marta had perished, but he never believed it. He attended the public hearing with the hope of finding her, but has been unsuccessful.

8.19. Fraternal twins, Yehudit Frank (Malek) and Solomon Malek. The twins were thirteen and a half years old when they entered the camp.

8.20. I photographed this picture of opposite-sex twins, Solomon and Yehudit Malek, at a young age; see photograph 8.19.

8.21. I photographed this picture of identical twins, Elias and Jacob Malek—younger siblings of Yehudit and Solomon Malek, shown in photographs 8.19 and 8.20.

8.22. The sign reads: "Looking for the son of David Mantzuli (could be Menchuly, Mentchuly, Manchuli or Mantchuly)—Mengele's twins. About 43 years old. His name is either Yoel (Joel) or Eli."
There is a pair of twins named Jacob and Elias Malek, who would have been 43 years old. It is possible that the family name was changed. These twins are shown in photograph 8.21.

8.23. Identical twins, Lia (Tchengari) Huber and Judit Barnea, were seated in the audience. These Romanian twins were part of Mengele's experiments, but did not testify at the Yad Vashem hearing.

8.24. Identical twins—audience, Yad Vashem hearing.

8.25. Fraternal twins, Rachel Simson (L) and Zehova Friedman, at the Yad Vashem hearing. The twins were twelve years old when they were held in the camp.

8.26. Rachel Simson (L) and and Zehava Friedman as young girls, at four or five years of age. I photographed this picture of the twins; see photograph 8.25.

8.27. Identical twins—Audience, Yad Vashem hearing.

8.28. Testimony of same-sex fraternal twin, Rivka Vered Mintz.
See Additional Annotation.

8.28. Rivka Vered Mintz claimed that Mengele was interested in her and in her twin sister because they were not identical. These twins were subjected to many experimental treatments, one involving eye drops. Rivka said that she has trouble seeing and had been told she has the "eyes of an old woman." Her twin sister became very sick and frail in the camps. On the day of the liberation and death march out of the camp, Rivka was informed that her sister would be taken by car—otherwise, she would not have left her. Her sister was never put in a car and did not survive.

8.29. Testimony of Eliza Baruch at the public hearing. She is not on the list of twins compiled by C.A.N.D.L.E.S., so may have been one of several nontwin survivors who testified.
See Additional Annotation.

8.29. Eliza Baruch arrived at Auschwitz at age fifteen and was placed with a group of twenty girls. She was told that one of her ovaries and half of her uterus had been removed, and she was subjected to radiation. "We became girls of four and five years old," she said. Four of Eliza's six children died at four days of age. Some of this information was provided in her testimony at Yad Vashem; also see Grodin, M. A., Kor, E., & Benedict, S. (2011). "The trial that never happened: Josef Mengele and the twins of Auschwitz." *War Crimes, Genocide, and Crimes Against Humanity*, 5(1 & 2), 3-90.

8.30. Identical twins, Hedvah (originally named Hojnol) and Leah Stern, who arrived at Auschwitz-Birkenau at age thirteen and a half. At the Jerusalem hearing, the twins were remembered for looking so much alike.
See Additional Annotation.

8.30. Following liberation, Hedvah and Leah Stern and other young Holocaust survivors founded *Moshav Nir-Galim,* a cooperative agricultural settlement near the sea, in Ashdod. *Nir-Galim* means "the air and the waves." Both twins married and had children and grandchildren. Lucette M. Lagnado and Sheila C. Dekel, *Children of the flames: Dr. Josef Mengele and the untold story of the twins of Auschwitz* (New York: William Morrow and Company, Inc., 1991).

8.31. Opposite-sex twins, Hova Brill and Moshe David, of Israel.

8.32. Testimony from opposite-sex twin Moshe David,
February 4, 2019. *See Additional Annotation.*

8.32. Moshe David, as a religious eleven-year-old, was among the first of the twins
to arrive at Auschwitz. During a selection he stood on his toes to appear taller
and older, but was unsuccessful. He was ordered to go to the death block, but the
decree was annulled.

8.33. Fraternal twins, Olga Solomon and Vera Kriegel, from Israel.
See Additional Annotation.

8.33. Vera Kriegel (R) arrived at Auschwitz at age five and was placed in a cage-like prison with her mother and fraternal twin sister, Olga (L). They were kept together because Mengele was fascinated by eye color, a trait that differed between the twins' mother and her twins. Vera recalled painful eye injections and described seeing a wall on which human eyes had been pinned like butterflies.

8.34. Fraternal twins, Vera Kriegel (L) and Olga Grossman,
twins' mother Shari, and Zvi Spiegel. At Yad Vashem.

8.35. Identical twins remembered for being a "beautiful" pair.
See Additional Annotation.

8.35. One of the twins (I believe her to be Leah Cuker Berkman) testified that experimental treatments, like radiation, probably caused her lungs to look like a "coal mine" later in life. She had always been a non-smoker.

8.36. Ruth Elias was a nontwin survivor whose only option was to put her newborn daughter to death to save her own life. Ruth was twenty-two years old at the time. Eventually she emigrated to Israel and started a family.

She appears in the 1985 documentary film *Shoah*, directed by the late Claude Lanzmann. Ruth Elias was the last person of thirty witnesses to testify.

8.37. Final Dinner, Holy Land Hotel, February 6, 1985.
L to R: Mrs. Lorenzcy, opposite-sex twin Menashe Lorenzcy, identical twin
Miriam Czaigher and misassigned fraternal twin Ephraim Reichenberg.

8.38. Simon Wiesenthal (R) seated next to a guest at the public hearing;
guest's identity is currently unknown. Final dinner, Holy Land Hotel,
February 6, 1985.

8.39. Yad Vashem panelists, Simon Wiesenthal (center L) and Telford Taylor, at Final Dinner. Holy Land Hotel, February 6, 1985.

8.40. Seated: Zvi Spiegel (L) and Peter Somogyi (fraternal twin in the group of young twin boys Spiegel helped bring home). Behind them are opposite-sex twin, René Slotkin and wife June. Final Dinner, Holy Land Hotel, February 6, 1985.

8.41. Twin Survivors, Yad Vashem, Jerusalem, Israel.
This picture is a composite of three photographs
I made of smaller groups of twins.
See Additional Annotation.

8.41. The twins are standing in the Yad Vashem Sculpture Park. Behind them is a reproduction of the Dachau memorial sculpture by Holocaust survivor and artist, Nandor Glid. The original work, installed in Dachau in 1967, "depicts extremely thin, angular and dislocated, deformed and tangled bodies." Glid was born in Subotica, Yugoslavia (now Serbia) in 1924 and passed away in 1997. The sculpture in its entirety can be viewed at https://www.army.mil/article/124542/travel_dachau_memorial_site_reveals_grim_chapter_of_world_history. Additional information about Nandor Glid's life and work can be found at https://www.etudier.com/dissertations/Nandor-Glid-M%C3%A9morial-De-Yad/48334311.html.

9. Aftermath: Inquiries and Inquest

The visit to Auschwitz-Birkenau and the Yad Vashem hearing solidified the bonds among the twins and gave them a common purpose: to find Josef Mengele and bring him to justice. That goal unraveled with the summer 1985 headlines announcing that Mengele had died six years earlier, in 1979. Forensic evidence pointed to the exhumed body as that of Mengele, but unanswered questions remained: Why did the bones show no signs of osteomyelitis, a condition Mengele had had as a child? Had the numerous sightings of Mengele since 1979 been fully investigated? Did the blood type of the alleged Nazi doctor's remains identify him as the father of his son, Rolf Mengele?[32,33]

Many twins were troubled at the thought that Mengele died in an ordinary drowning accident, under the name Wolfgang Gerhard. They thought that, surely, he must have arranged for another body to take his place, leaving him free to work and travel.

In response to the unexpected news and the considerable controversy raised by some of the findings, Eva Kor organized the event "C.A.N.D.L.E.S. Inquest: The Truth About Mengele." Its purpose was to review the forensic evidence and to gather additional testimony from twins who had not attended the public hearing in Jerusalem. Experts in forensic analysis, history, law, and other disciplines were invited to the three-day event in Terre Haute, Indiana.

---

32 Growing up, Rolf Mengele was told that his father was his uncle ("Uncle Fritz"). Rolf Mengele has been a lawyer in West Germany. David G. Marwell, D.G. (2020), *Mengele: Unmasking the Angel of Death* (New York, W.W. Norton & Co. 2020); Gerald L. Posner & John Ware, *Mengele: The Complete Story* (New York: McGraw Hill Book Co., 1986).

33 Mengele did not get a blood-type tattoo as did other Nazis. Caroline Howe, "Nazi 'Angel of Death' Doctor Josef Mengele was Obsessed with Dwarfism and Twins but his Choice 'Specimen' was a 12-Year-Old Boy's Head He Planned to Dissect, New Book on his Monstrosities Reveal." Daily Mail, https://www.dailymail.co.uk/news/article-8012697/Nazi-Josef-Mengeles-choice-specimen-12-year-old-boys-head-planned-dissect-lab.html, February 18, 2020. However, blood type cannot prove paternity even if the blood types of the alleged father and son are compatible; it can only assign paternity with a level of certainty. That is because two unrelated individuals can share blood groups by chance, rather than by descent. However, when rare blood groups are shared by alleged relatives and multiple blood groups are examined, the probability of their genetic relatedness increases.

The Inquest would take place at the Hulman Center, a 10,200-seat arena, located on the campus of Indiana State University.[34]

I chaired a panel that addressed the psychological and emotional effects of being a twin child in the camp and a twin survivor later in life. Panel members included Drs. Auke Tellegen (University of Minnesota, Minneapolis), David Guttman (Northwestern University, Chicago), David Leventhal (Case Western Reserve University) and Robert Nathan (Hahnemann Medical University, Philadelphia).

A press release about the event was distributed in advance of the Inquest. In truth, I was apprehensive about holding this important event in a small, difficult to reach midwestern city in November when weather is uncertain. Given the widespread interest and significance of the topic—and the fact that the news of Mengele's death was relatively recent and highly provocative—a more appropriate venue would have been New York City, Chicago, Los Angeles or other large, easily accessible city, and a more suitable time would have been early spring. Looking at the photographs of presenters David G. Marwell, John Loftus, and Michael Baden, one can see that they are surrounded by rows of empty seats. Unfortunately, attendees filled only the first two rows of the large auditorium and there was little press coverage. Nevertheless, the Inquest was an informative and meaningful experience for everyone in attendance—it brought surviving twins together with experts from diverse disciplines, combining scientific findings with human stories.

Surviving twin Vera Kriegel unveiled her original poem, "The Bell of Freedom!" Her composition adds to a long tradition of such works by individuals dedicated to the many meanings of freedom and independence over the ages.[35] I have reproduced her words exactly as they were written:

The Bell of Freedom!

From this Holy City

We're ringing a Bell
A Bell of Freedom
Which was bought in Hell—

---

34 Indiana State University, "Conferences and Event Services." http://venues.indstate.edu/isuvenue/the-hulman-center-main-activity-floor/, accessed May 2022.

35 Oliver Tearle, "10 of the Best Poems about Freedom and Liberty." *Interesting Literature,* https://interestingliterature.com/2020/05/freedom-poems-liberty-liberation/, 2022.

World stand still listen and hear
Do you hear it loud and clear?

For our Freedom

We paid a price so high,
With six million stars
There in the sky
They shine upon us
But we ask why?
Why dear God
Did so many have to die?

We want the World to join us

In our plead for heed—
When if not now
In this hour of need?
World remember the Past—
For a Better Future,
Otherwise we shall lose
The Old Mother Nature

Dear Lord!

Listen to our Ringing Bell
Which we bought
And we shall never sell.
For we need it
To remind the World—
Now in the clutches of Death
We constantly curled.

But somehow,

We made it.
And proudly
We stand here in Unity,
Ringing our Bell
For a Better Destiny

ISRAEL, Sept. 1985

By Vera Kriegel (Mengele's Twin)

The Panel issued a statement at the conclusion of the event, signed by all seven members: Eva Kor, Dr. Nancy Segal, Tony van Renterghem, Barbara Weymouth, Gerald Posner, Esq., Dr. Werner Loewenstein, and Dr. Richard Pierard. Some key excerpts from that document follow:

- "We cannot close the door on the Mengele case."
- "We agree with the forensics experts that their preliminary report is not complete."
- " . . . this Panel recommends that C.A.N.D.L.E.S. and its representatives be included in any future preparation of reports and analyses relating to the possible death of Josef Mengele."

It was not until 1992 that the necessary sophisticated analytic procedure of DNA fingerprinting from the exhumed skeletal bones and blood from Mengele's son, Rolf, and wife, Irene, was possible. The results confirmed that Josef Mengele was Rolf's father with a very high degree of certainty.[36] This finding settled the question of Mengele's death for many members of the scientific community and general public, but some scientists, twins, and government officials were not convinced. It was also recognized that acceptance by some of these individuals would be unlikely unless the government of Israel agreed.[37]

For now, the formal investigation of Dr. Josef Mengele's whereabouts is over, but in the minds of some people it is unfinished. The case remains unsettled for many who were intent upon bringing the Angel of Death to justice. It would not be surprising to learn that efforts to find him are continuing quietly in the United States, Germany, and especially Israel.

---

36 Jeffreys, A. J., Allen, M. J., Hagelberg, E., & Sonnberg, A. (1992). Identification of the skeletal remains of Josef Mengele by DNA analysis. *Forensic Science International*, 56 (1), 65-76.

37 David G. Marwell, *Mengele: Unmasking the Angel of Death* (New York: W.W. Norton & Co., 2020).

9.1. The C.A.N.D.L.E.S. Inquest took place in Terre Haute, Indiana—nine months after the Yad Vashem hearing and five months after the death of Dr. Josef Mengele was announced.

Additional Sources (Section 9):
https://www.davidgmarwell.com/
https://web.archive.org/web/20030604055731/http://john-loftus.com/bio.asp
https://www.drmichaelbaden.com/bio/

9.2. I photographed this picture of Helen Rapaport (L) and Pearle Pufules (Herskovic) as young twins, holding their toys. The identity of the women standing next to them (who appear to be twins) is unknown.

9.3. Arnold (brother) and identical twins, Pearle and Helen Herskovic, in Zatec, Czechoslovakia, 1945.

The twins are twenty-three years of age in this picture that I photographed—they arrived at Auschwitz-Birkenau shortly thereafter.

9.4. Identical twins, Helen Rapaport (L) of Skokie, IL, and Pearle Pufules (Herskovic) of Joliet, IL. Helen was diagnosed with tuberculosis as an adult, a likely effect of the medical experimentation she had undergone. These twins attended the Inquest, but were not present at the Auschwitz-Birkenau gathering or the Yad Vashem hearing.

9.5. Surviving identical twin, Frank Klein (seated)
with Inquest panelist, Dr. Werner Loewenstein.

9.6. Dr. David G. Marwell, historian and former director
of New York City's Museum of Jewish Heritage. He is the author
of *Mengele: Unmasking the Angel of Death* (2020). Dr. Marwell
testified at the Inquest.

9.7. John Loftus, former high-level U.S. government prosecutor, Army intelligence officer and Nazi-hunter. Loftus authored *The Belarus Secret* (1982) and *The Secret War Against the Jews* (1997), co-written with Mark Aarons. Both books claim various connections between the Nazis and the CIA, FBI and other government bodies in the United States and western countries. John Loftus testified at the Inquest.

9.8. Dr. Michael Baden, forensic pathologist, has investigated the deaths of many high-profile individuals. He served as Chief Medical Examiner of New York City from 1978 to 1979. Dr. Baden appeared for thirteen years on his own HBO television series *Autopsy*. He testified at the Inquest.

9.9. Former Dutch Resistance fighter and Research Director for C.A.N.D.L.E.S., Tony van Renterghem (L), and attorney Gerald Posner. Posner is holding the Conclusion reached by the panel on the final day of the Inquest. It was signed by the seven Panel members.

10. Twin Children of the Holocaust: After the Public Hearing and Beyond

On June 23, 1985, Irene Hizme and her husband, Sam, hosted a gathering of twins and families at their home in Oceanside, Long Island. It was an opportunity to meet many people we had heard about who did not attend the events in Poland and Israel—among them, Peter Somogyi's father Joseph, and René and Irene's adoptive mother, Dinah. It was also a chance to meet many of the twins' children who exist only because of their parents' twinship, resourcefulness, and luck. These children will help preserve the memories of their parents across the generations to come.

As time went by, I reconnected with some of the twins. I was delighted to be in touch with Peter and Anna Somogyi, whom I had first met at the Slotkins' home in December 1984. In November 2014, I would be traveling to Budapest, Hungary for a conference and remembered that Peter was from a small Hungarian town. Fortunately, he was still living at the same address in White Plains, New York, so I was able to contact him. He told me he was from Pécs and suggested I find his childhood home, his family's Holocaust memorial and the city's synagogue—now a world monument.[38] Peter and Anna also helped me reconnect with Peter's brother, Tom.

Several years ago, I learned that Irene was invited to discuss her experiences and show her film, *Rene and I: From Auschwitz to America*, at Chapman University, in Orange County, California where I live and work.[39] I attended that event and waited until Irene was no longer surrounded by the many interested individuals asking her questions. When she was finally alone, I approached her, and we enjoyed a wonderful, warm reunion. Several months later, when I was in New York, we met at her home in Oceanside and discussed the exciting possibility of transcribing the audio tapes I had made of the twins' testi-

---

38   Synagogues360. "Pecs Synagogue." https://synagogues-360.anumuseum.org.il/gallery/pecs-synagogue/, 2022.

39   Angelone, G.M., Director (2005). *Rene and I: From Auschwitz to America* (New York: Twin Pix Production, LLC).

mony at Yad Vashem. We soon learned that that job had already been completed—however, no one had ever published pictures from the visit to Poland or the public hearing.

In October 1994, I received a letter from identical twin Stephanie (Stepha) Heller saying that she and her sister, Annetta, had learned about my research in an Australian newsletter for twins and would be happy to see me in Melbourne where they lived. I had met them at the public hearing at Yad Vashem. Ten years later, as I was planning my book *Indivisible by Two: Lives of Extraordinary Twins*, I believed it would be important to include them. I spent several days with the twins and their families for a chapter titled, *Two Bodies and One Soul.*[40] Another ten years passed until I saw them again—this time, I was invited to speak at a conference, *Healthier Kids: Insights From Twin Research*, at the Royal Children's Hospital, in Melbourne. It was a wonderful opportunity to invite them to the book signing and to share a celebratory drink at the hotel.

As I was completing this book, I asked Annetta to compose a tribute to her twin sister, Stepha, who had passed away several years before. Her words could have been written by any of the twins of Auschwitz-Birkenau:

> My twin sister, Stepha, and I were inseparable for 95 years until her passing in September 2019. As Jews we were rounded up and sent to Theresienstadt and then to Auschwitz in December 1943, where being identical twins brought us to Dr. Mengele's attention and the unthinkable medical experiments that followed. This saved our lives, but not that of the rest of our family. Being twins has meant we always had: a sister, a friend, a supporter, a mentor, and a critic. My sister was my everything and I loved her deeply and miss her every day.

Annetta and Stepha were truly *two bodies and one soul*. I cannot take credit for these words which I used as the title of their chapter in my book *Indivisible by Two*—when one of the twins described their relationship in that way, I knew it was perfect.

---

40 Nancy L. Segal, *Indivisible by two: Lives of extraordinary twins* (Cambridge, MA: Harvard University Press, 2005/2007).

10.1. Sometime after the Yad Vashem hearing, fraternal twin Irene Hizme (R) reunited with her friend, Miriam Altman, from the Paris orphanage in which she was placed several years after the liberation of Auschwitz-Birkenau. Recall that Irene passed away in May 2019.

10.2. Fraternal twins, René Slotkin (L) and Irene Hizme, both married twins—June Slotkin and Samuel Hizme, respectively. Irene and Sam held a gathering of Holocaust twins and their families at their home in Oceanside, Long Island on June 23, 1985—four months after the public hearing, and several weeks after news of Mengele's death was announced.

10.3. Joseph (Izso) Somogyi (L), father of twins Peter and Tom Somogyi, with René Slotkin. June 1985 gathering of twins on Long Island. Joseph passed away in 2003.

10.4. Joseph (Izso) Somogyi (L) with guest Bill Hodges who studied the Nazi underground in South America. On the sofa between them is the weekly German publication Bunte ("Colorful"), a celebrity magazine that launched a series on Josef Mengele and his son Rolf in mid-June 1985. Hodges also spoke with René's wife, June Slotkin, about René's experiences at Auschwitz. June 1985 gathering of twins on Long Island.

10.5. Sam Hizme (L), Irene's husband, with twin Peter Somogyi,
son of Joseph Somogyi shown in photographs 10.3 and 10.4,
at the June 1985 gathering of twins on Long Island.

10.6. Fraternal twin Peter Greenfeld (L), and fraternal twin René Slotkin, examining childhood photographs. I photographed this "picture of a picture" at the Long Island gathering—it was originally taken by a person named "Louis" in Israel, February 1985. Note: The twin in the small photograph on the right is René at age 11, about one year before going to America. The small photograph on the left is from the film footage of the liberation of the children by the Soviet military. It is hard to see, but René is holding the hand of a Czech artist, a dwarfed inmate who was housed with René. Also see photographs 5.3 and 5.5–5.6.

10.7. Andrea (Peter and Anna Somogyi's daughter, L) and mother Anna at the June 1985 gathering of twins on Long Island.

10.8. Mrs. Charlotte Somogyi, Joseph Somogyi's second wife (L), and Mrs. Dinah Slotkin, adoptive mother of twins Irene and René. The women are discussing events surrounding the twins' adoption.

10.9. June Slotkin (L) and daughter Mia with her mother-in-law, Dinah (Rosen) Slotkin, the woman who adopted twins Irene and René. June 1985 gathering of twins on Long Island.

10.10. Identical twins, Annetta Able (L) and Stephanie (Stepha) Heller (R), with Nancy L. Segal (center), December 2014.
We are celebrating being together again—our previous meeting was in December 2004 when I visited Melbourne to interview the twins for my book, *Indivisible by Two: Lives of Extraordinary Twins*.
We are seated in the lounge of Melbourne, Australia's Rydges Hotel.
This photograph was taken by Annetta's son, Danny, who joined us.

10.11. I attended the 15th International Congress on Twin Studies, in Budapest, Hungary, November 2014. Fraternal twin Peter Somogyi, suggested I visit his hometown of Pécs, located approximately 150 miles to the south of the capital city. Shown here is the home where Peter and his twin brother Tom grew up.

10.12. This photograph shows the Somogyi family gravestone. Albert was Peter and Tom's grandfather; their grandmother Olga is not shown. Somogyi Izsone (née Eisner Erzsebet) was Peter and Tom's mother and Somogyi Alice was their sister. Peter's father Joseph (Izso), shown in photographs 10.3 and 10.4, had inscriptions made of the names of his family members who perished at Auschwitz.

10.13. The original synagogue in Pécs, Hungary (1865) that has been rebuilt and remodeled. On display are photographs of rabbis, families, personal artifacts, and documents providing historical accounts of the Jewish community of Pécs. The Hebrew words at the top read, "The House of Worship for all People" (Isaiah 56:7). Above that is a replica of the Mosaic tablets showing the Ten Commandments. Below is a clock with Roman numerals.

Parting Words

It was gratifying to finally compile my photographs of the twin children of the Holocaust into this book. Leafing through the five albums in which the pictures were stored rekindled memories of my first meeting with the twins, the visit to Auschwitz-Birkenau, the public hearing at Yad Vashem and the different events that followed those extraordinary experiences. As a professor of psychology, I attend many academic conferences, but I have never been to one as professionally significant and as personally meaningful as these gatherings of twin survivors.

Working on this book has given me new appreciation for the power of pictures. I have never been trained in photography—yet, outfitted with my new Nikon camera, my intention was to capture as many people, places, and events that I could. I pressed the button wildly, hoping for the best. The pictures vary in quality—I believe the one showing twins Eva and Miriam standing before their childhood images at the time of liberation (5.3) stands out for its uniqueness. The gathering of twins and their families for prayer and song at Auschwitz-Birkenau (4.10) needed better lighting—but their mission of remembrance and their spirit of unity are clear. Some pictures of the twins as children prior to their camp arrival appear fragile and faded (8.17 and 8.26), but are treasured tokens of happier times and have been reproduced as such.

My hope is that these photographs, both individually and collectively, will deepen our understanding of this tragic episode in human history.

Acknowledgments

Every book is a partnership. I have many people to thank for their contributions and support as I completed the different sections of *The Twin Children of the Holocaust.*

- I will begin with Alessandra Anzani, Editorial Director of Academic Studies Press (ASP). Alessandra understood the significance of the twins' photographs when I contacted her about this project, and gave me the extraordinary opportunity to turn them into an annotated collection. The other staff at ASP, especially Kira Nemirovsky, Production Manager, have been wonderfully helpful throughout the entire process.

- My boyfriend, Dr. Craig K. Ihara, reviewed every selection of text as he does with each book that I write. His invaluable insights, perspectives and comments made this work a document of which I am proud. Craig is also a wonderful dancer, a benefit that provided many relaxed, joyful moments that were greatly needed as I completed this book.

- I think of graphic artist (and identical twin) Kelly Donovan as a magician! Kelly edited every photograph that needed editing, bringing her unusual artistic talents to the fore.

- I am indebted to Zuzanna Janusik (Head of Exhibitions) and Agnieszka Sieradzka (Art Historian and Curator of Collections) at the Auschwitz-Birkenau State Museum for providing details about the artwork included in this book.

- My wonderful graduate student friends, Dr. Elisha Klirs and his wife, Rabbi Tracy Guren Klirs, provided translations of some Hebrew words and phrases.

- I am grateful to have received a grant from California State University, Fullerton (Office of Research and Sponsored Projects), for the support of scholarly or creative productivity.

- I saved my final words of gratitude for the twins and their families whose enthusiasm and support overwhelm me still. You were always kind and generous despite the many questions I posed to you over the past year. Because of your efforts, these photographs will be seen by future generations whose responsibilities will be to acknowledge, to understand, and to prevent.

About the Author

Dr. Nancy L. Segal is professor of psychology at California State University, Fullerton, and director of the Twin Studies Center. She has authored over 300 articles and eight books on many topics involving twins and their development. Her 2012 book, *Born Together—Reared Apart: The Landmark Minnesota Twin Study*, won the 2013 William James Book Award from the American Psychological Association; her other books are listed on the page that follows. Dr. Segal has appeared on *CBS This Morning*, *CNN*, and the *Oprah Winfrey Show*, and her work has been featured in the *New York Times* and *Wall Street Journal*. She has received a number of international awards, including the *James Shields Award for Lifetime Contributions to Twin Research* (International Society for Twin Studies) and the *International Making a Difference Award* (Multiple Births Canada). Her 2021 book, *Deliberately Divided: Inside the Controversial Study of Twins and Triplets Adopted Apart*, was the focus of a *BBC World News* documentary film, aired in July 2022 on television stations worldwide. Her 2023 book, *Gay Fathers—Twin Sons: The Citizenship Case That Captured the World*, examines a high-profile lawsuit that combined the timely themes of same-sex marriage, citizenship, surrogacy, family and, of course, twinship. Dr. Segal lives and works in southern California.

Please visit Dr. Nancy L. Segal's website—drnancysegaltwins.org—for her calendar of events, as well as her articles, reviews, photographs, and other twin-related material.

Photo Credit: Tony Kawashima

Other Books by Nancy L. Segal

Entwined Lives: Twins and What They Tell Us About Human Behavior (2000)

Indivisible by Two: Lives of Extraordinary Twins (2007)

Someone Else's Twin: The True Story of Babies Switched at Birth (2011)

Born Together—Reared Apart: The Landmark Minnesota Twin Study (2012)

Twin Mythconceptions: False Beliefs, Fables, and Facts About Twins (2017)

Accidental Brothers: The Story of Twins Exchanged at Birth and the Power of Nature and Nurture (2018, co-author: Y.S. Montoya)

Deliberately Divided: Inside the Controversial Study of Twins and Triplets Adopted Apart (2021)

Gay Fathers—Twin Sons: The Citizenship Case That Captured the World (2023)

Edited Volumes

Uniting Psychology and Biology: Integrative Perspectives on Human Development (1997; co-editors: N.L. Segal, G.E. Weisfeld and C.C. Weisfeld)

Twin Research for Everyone: From Biology to Health, Epigenetics, and Psychology (2022; co-editors: A.D. Tarnoki, D.L. Tarnoki, J.R. Harris, and N.L. Segal)